KUDOS

If you'd like a jumpstart on the art of conversation with your kids, Billy Sprague has got the book for you! In conversational warmth and honesty, Billy sits across the table from you and shares his life experiences, missteps and victories. He helps lead the way for you to open up to your own kids with your deepest hopes, dreams and prayers for their growth and development. These conversations are vital. Hurry and get your copy. Your kids will be grown soon!

> Nan Gurley – portrayed Corrie ten Boom
> in the movie The Hiding Place, 2023

Very few people actually capture the truly important out of a world of "non-importants." Billy Sprague is one of those that does. In Sacred vs. Shinola, Billy spotlights the important...the essentials for making great parents out of good parents, and helps direct the focus of Moms and Dads to what is crucial for raising healthy teens in today's culture.

> Mark Gregston – Founder of Heartlight, a residential
> counseling center for teens

Such an enjoyable recounting of the journey of a loving father and his children through their growing-up years. Billy's honesty is refreshing, as he unpacks their wonderful and sometimes imperfect family life together. His letters underscore the resilience of kids as well as the grace that God bestows on us as parents. Through humorous anecdotes and compelling illustrations, we're implored to take up the challenge of exposing the dangerous counterfeits of our culture that seek to rob us and our kids of growing in true character and Christlikeness.

> Larry Zimbelman – Executive Director FlatIrons Academy
> Westminster, Colorado

SACRED VS. SHINOLA

Letters to my children from the kitchen table

Billy Sprague

Out of the Bluebell Publishing

TABLE OF CONTENTS

Awareness of the sacred in life is what holds our world together, and the lack of awareness of the sacred is what is tearing it apart.

Sister Joan Chittister

NOTE FROM THE AUTHOR

Two things sparked these letters. A song I recorded five years before our first blessing, Willow, arrived. *When Nothing's Sacred.* Here's the lyric:

People need true love - But chase infatuation
They need a hope - But live on short supply
People need wisdom - But get more education
People need forgiveness - But settle things eye for eye
People need identity - But are satisfied with titles
They need true courage - But bravado looks sincere
People need a living God - But seem content with idols
People need a destiny - But settle for careers

CHORUS
And the soul remains unsettled, And the world a wilderness
In a time when nothing's sacred, And souls settle for less

People need faith - But place their bets on science
They need a refuge - But stay out in the rain
People need each other - But rely on self-reliance

People need a Christmas - But settle for a holiday
People need dignity - But survive on ego
They need the Truth - But will take an alibi
People need a Savior - But much prefer a hero
Most long for heaven - But have settled for the sky

CHORUS
And the soul remains unsettled, And the world a wilderness
In a time when nothing's sacred, And souls settle for less

© Skin Horse, Inc. 1993 by Billy Sprague

You can listen to it in a Spotify playlist via the QR code below, as well as other songs quoted and referred to in these letters.

The other spark was one of our favorite shows, Andy Griffith. An episode called "Opie's Hobo Friend" presents a dilemma for Sheriff Taylor's young son, Opie. Andy's wisdom got my ink flowing in my first letter, Sacred vs. Shinola.

Letter 1

Sacred vs. *Shinola*

My dear children,

To begin, I have a confession.

Over the course of my life, in the pursuit of the things that matter most, the sacred stuff, I have often settled for Shinola.

What is Shinola? (pronounced shī nō' luh) Originally, it was a shoe polish first manufactured in 1877. In one of those moments when wit collided with wisdom in some crusty farmer's head, Shinola slid into a colorful expression coined even before I was born. The old saying contains a word I prefer you don't frequently use. However, in this rare and specific case, it's part of the expression I need to make my point. The word is a crude synonym for dung or manure. The old saying goes like this, "That guy doesn't know s—t from Shinola." I know. That's a little too fun to say out loud and repeat to your friends. Try to contain yourselves.

This coarse and less-than-flattering observation was aimed at someone who has extremely poor judgment and even less sense. Its target is someone who cannot tell the difference between cow crap and a greasy paste meant to put a new shine on shoes. Someone would have to be pretty thickheaded to mistake a fresh, steamy cow paddy for shoe polish.

I want to borrow half of that old saying and turn it another way. Remarkably, people often don't know Sacred from Shinola. That seems truer today than ever. People everywhere, including you and me, fall for things that are shined up and sold to look authentic, solid, and satisfying. When the deal doesn't deliver, we feel let down, sometimes even deceived. Settling for Shinola instead of Sacred is the source of a lot of disappointment and brokenness in the world.

The only upside to settling for less is this: it can awaken our longing and search for what *is* true, lasting and soul-satisfying. Deep down we are made for the pure gold, but can easily mistake pyrite, fool's gold, for the real thing. As another old saying goes, "All that glitters is not gold." Likewise, all that is shiny is not sacred.

Truth be known, there were times I could have been the poster child for that farmer's colorful saying. Honestly, I can't even say I was always looking for the real thing, the sacred, especially early on. Maybe the pure longing for what really mattered was buried many layers beneath my daily pursuits and appetites. But most of the time, I just wanted Shinola, a quick fix, a bird in the hand, a high-gloss, tangible, unsatisfying substitute for the sacred. Maybe that's just part of being young and naïve, but even that excuse has some Shinola on it.

My personal failings make your presence in my life an even more awesome act of divine grace and mercy. I don't deserve the sacred honor of being your Dad. I am beyond grateful.

By speaking my heart in ink to you my hope is this: that you will fall for Shinola less than I did - that you will not give in as easily to the lure of what is often a shimmering mirage, sometimes

2

maybe even a good thing, but not the best - and I pray you will train your eyes and set your heart on what really matters, and be less scarred and more blessed.

I also hope you will not adopt a defensive style of keeping the world at arm's length; after all, this world is God's magnificent creation and holds great beauty and goodness and glory. My highest hope is that you develop an appetite for something deeper, a passion for what is real, of true value, and which is always stirring below the surface of everyday life and within everyone you meet.

* * *

From my vantage point just a little farther down the road from you, I want to prepare you for some of the Shinola peddlers you will meet, much like an early TV character Andy Griffith does for his son Opie.

We love the episode where a drifter, played by Buddy Ebsen, "adjusts" Opie's value system. (Season 2, episode 6, titled "Opie's Hobo Friend") The hobo instructs Andy's son in the fine art of living off the land, like "borrowing", actually, stealing pies and chickens. He puts off work till tomorrow if there is fishing to be done today and "frees" gumballs from the machine with only a magic word, 'Tuscarora," and a pry tool kept cleverly out of sight. Andy, a wise father, confronts him. The drifter catches his drift. But not without a typical Shinola rebuttal.

Andy: It's about Opie.
Hobo: Something wrong?

Andy: Well, there seems to be something wrong with
       Opie's thinkin'. He's gotten a little twisted
       on things lately, like being able to tell the
       difference between right and wrong. Not that
       that's an easy thing, there's a lot of grownups still
       strugglin' with that same problem, but it's
       especially difficult for a youngster, cause things rub
       off on 'em so easy.

Hobo: I see, are you suggestin' I may be not too fit
       company for Opie?

Andy: That would seem the case.

Hobo: Well, Sheriff, maybe I do look at things a little
       different than other people. Is that wrong? I live by
       my wits. I'm not above bendin' the law now and
       then to keep clothes on my back or food in my
       stomach. I live the kind of life other people would just
       love to live if they only had the courage. Who's to say
       that the boy would be happier your way or mine?
       Why not let him decide?

Andy: No, I'm afraid it don't work 'at way. You can't let a
       young'un decide for himself. He'll grab
       the first flashy thing with shiny ribbons on it. Then
       when he finds out there's a hook in it, it's too late.
       Wrong ideas come packaged with so much glitter it's
       hard to convince 'em that other things might be better in
       the long run. And all a parent can do is say, 'wait'
       and 'trust me' and try to keep temptation away.

Hobo: That means that you're inviting me to leave?

Andy: That's right.

Hobo: Well, You're wearin' the badge so - I leave -. That wasn't so difficult. Your problem's solved.

Andy: That's where you're wrong. That boy thinks just about everything you do is perfect. So, my problem's just beginning. You've left behind an awful lot of unscramblin' to be done.

The hobo is, in fact, a Shinola peddler, just one of the many you will run into. He is apparently a harmless, even likable fellow, like most you will meet. But he is a master of the old verbal sleight of hand. He shamelessly trots out the noble word "courage" to whitewash his bravado. (More on that in the letter: Courage vs. Bravado.) He drapes his own selfishness in a flag of freedom, which gives him a license to blur the lines between another man's chicken and his own needs. And perhaps the oldest shell game of them all - he flies his highest banner, "happiness" - his own, as the best reason for the way he lives. (See the letter: Joy vs. Happiness.)

Today, personal happiness is widely accepted as one of the chief purposes and rights of life. Talk about a terrible candidate for a musketeer - the hobo's motto is obvious: "All for one and the one is me." Is it any wonder he's a drifter and alone?

Andy has seen this type of values mangler and steps in. You see, my too-soon-grown-and-flown fledglings, Sheriff Taylor knows that freedom without a moral compass is just another form of slavery - slavery to self. (See the letter: Usie vs. Selfie) This self-centered condition can cause complete blindness to the worth and dignity of the other person whose chicken or parking space, spouse or hard-earned dollar is taken for one's own personal agenda. As a sheriff and a father his job is to protect and to serve. So, that's what Andy does in his wise and direct way.

For some time now, to protect and serve you, your mother and I have done most of the deciding. Early on, we did nearly all of it. For a season, the word you probably heard most from us was, "No."

You will soon do all the deciding for yourselves. All along the way, you will run into a lot of flashy things polished up in Shinola, buffed to a high gloss, and passed off as the real deal, new and improved. You will be made to doubt if you can live, and be truly happy, successful, secure, "modern" or smart without it. And you will have to decide.

My hope is that you will see these fakes for what they are – less than essential, far less than sacred – and you will not settle for less, as much I have – and choose the best – better and sooner than I did.

By divine help and trial and error, I hope you will see through the glitter and the slick pitch from a hobo or huckster, a politician or preacher, a pretty face or the most powerful of them all – the little Goliath living inside your head. This one rarely sleeps, tries to appear so reliable and loyal, and always argues eloquently for your best interest. This constant companion is a majority partner in the law firm of My, Me and Mine – your strongest, most persistent and resourceful ally – your "self," sometimes called our "ego". (More on that in the letter: Dignity vs. Ego)

Do I think you will perfectly apply all of what you take from any insight carved from my experience? Of course not. Unfortunately, blind spots, like many other things I've passed on to you, are embedded in your genes. Fortunately, unlike the leopard, we can, with God's help, change our spots. An English poet wrote:

"To err is human; to forgive divine." Alexander Pope

Many of the things I tell you in these pages may not ring true until you settle for less in some area, and feel very painfully the let down or sting of your choice. I fully expect you will sometimes learn from the hollow feeling or hunger that prowls within you after choosing the dazzle of temporary satisfactions or a less than genuine thing or person - over solid, sacred realities. Far too often, this old Latin saying is true.

"Experienta est magister ultimum" (Roman proverb)
Experience is the best teacher.

I hope some of what I offer here moves you along faster and farther. That your sight and insight will be keener than mine to sniff out Shinola better. To sense sooner what is sacred, and choose it more decisively. I hope your journey will be less driven by external winds or internal, momentary cravings, and instead be guided more by an early passion for the holy treasures of life.

I hope all this because one of the most sacred things to me - is you - and the condition and outcome of your soul and spirit. Come what may, you have my unshakable love and support. All I ask is that you consider the following as traveling notes, offered from someone who is cheering and praying for you. As you set your own courses for life, liberty, and the pursuit of what really matters, I pray something in these letters helps you walk more confidently into the future, whatever life throws in your path, and onto your shoes.

Love, Dad

Letter 2

Faith vs. *Fate*

Faith is taking the first step when you don't see the whole staircase.

Martin Luther King, Jr.

My fresh canvases,

Since you could talk, you have each blurted out pure nuggets. Most of the time it was flakes of golden delight.

Willow, at age five, you wondered if 'supervision' meant you could see through things, and if 'kindergarten' meant you had to garden there. Wyatt, some nights in your bed you sang over and over again, "God is bigger than the boogie man. God is bigger than the boogie man." One sunny weekend, we drove out into the country for a bluegrass festival. Parking was in a big green pasture. You blurted out, as serious as you could be, "Where is all the *blue* grass?" Hysterical. And Sawyer, you didn't need to know grammar to communicate effectively. When you were thirsty, all you had to say was, "I super drinky." And when you got in trouble, your masterful defense was, "I just a kid."

Sometimes, however, the nuggets were loaded with timely wisdom.

Wyatt, about the time you turned six, we took a walk around the block. Our family was facing a big decision, to leave Nashville after twenty-five years for steadier work than writing songs and making music. It was extremely difficult for all of us, leaving our home and friends. Except for you Sawyer. You were only a few months old.

I had interviewed to lead worship and music in a handful of places: Dallas, Austin, Orlando and Denver. As we walked, I said I needed you to pray about where the Lord wanted us to go.

Without hesitating you said, "God is everywhere, Daddy. Why don't you go where you want?"

I laughed. Stopped. And said, "That's the best advice I've heard."

You followed up immediately with, "God must be really fat to be everywhere." We had such a good laugh.

I actually told that story in a job interview. They wondered if they had a chance of hiring me against a position in Colorado. Nope. That's where we went. It turned out to be more than a good choice.

Was the decision (a) fate? in the stars? (b) a careful choice made from a list of pros and cons?, or (c) a path we were guided to by a divine assistance?

The word "fate" implies some nebulous force operating like gravity to direct our lives. It brings blessing or disaster. It's a force as unfeeling as math, a kind of predetermined blueprint or algorithm baked into the universe. (*Algorithm* is a fancy word for a set of operating rules, like the operating system, OS, in a computer.) You'll find the word "fate" in songs like "Have Yourself a Merry Little Christmas."

Through the years we all will be together –
If the FATES allow

10

The FATES? That sounds like a faceless board of directors determining who lives, who dies, who's happy and who's not.

The ancient Greeks put faces and names on the Fates. Clotho was a spinner of thread. She spun the thread of each person's life. Lachesis allotted the thread to each person. And Atropos, depicted as an old woman, determined when a person died by cutting the thread. The Greeks came up with fanciful and poetic storytelling to explain the nature of life and the universe. That's interesting, but we know a different story. Not a made up one. We don't have to invent stories about who gives us life and knows our path.

Psalm 139 puts our story well. Here's just some of it. Verses 13 – 16

> For you created my inmost being;
> you knit me together in my mother's womb.
> I praise you because I am fearfully and wonderfully made;
> your works are wonderful,
> I know that full well.
> My frame was not hidden from you
> when I was made in the secret place,
> when I was woven together in the depths of the earth.
> Your eyes saw my unformed body;
> all the days ordained for me were written in your book
> before one of them came to be.

As a songwriter, I've always wondered if the songwriter who wrote "Have Yourself a Merry Little Christmas" considered writing, "if the Lord allows" instead of "if the Fates allow." After all, it's a song for the season that celebrates the incarnation of our divine Maker, Redeemer and Overseer. Doesn't it seem much harder to be merry in a universe where life is a crap shoot, determined by impersonal forces that may or may not "allow" us to be with the ones we love? Am I overthinking it? Is it just a casual phrase in a lovely song and I should just have another spiked eggnog and party on?

I don't think so. Especially for your sake.

My charming elves, you will come face to face with many big decisions in life. To start something, marry someone, or not, stay somewhere or leave for somewhere else. Some decisions will be agonizing and life-altering. You will battle uncertainty and doubt - the "what ifs." What if I choose wrong? What if it doesn't work out? No matter how thorough your list of pros and cons, it will always boil down to an element of faith. Not fate. You will choose.

But here's where having a divine Overseer gives you what fictional Greek little 'g' gods, karma, astrology and horoscope readings are powerless to give. No matter what direction you choose, remember this, my little explorers.

The mind of man plans his way, but the Lord directs his steps.
Proverbs 16:9

Read that again. Breathe it in. What a relief, right? So, what if you choose wrong? What if a road, a plan, doesn't work out?

More than a few times, I have left everything behind in my life. Sometimes by my choice. Sometimes as a result of the choice of someone else. Never by fate. And always under the watchful care and guidance of the Big Picture Maker.

12

Here's another of your nuggets that more than hints that faith trumps fate.

One day, driving down the road, Willow, you and Wyatt were in the back seat.

Willow, you said, "Daddy, could God give me blue wings?"

That mix of curiosity and whimsy was so delightful. I tried to answer in the same style. "Sure, God can do anything. He could probably cut them out of the sky."

Wyatt, you chimed in. I knew your Sunday school was going through the creation story.

You said with great confidence, "No. All he would have to say is 'Let there be blue.'"

Mind blown! Pure joy. I hope to have that kind of faith someday.

It was more than fate that brought us together. That allows us to be together. Remember my golden nuggets: We plan. We choose. God directs our steps.

I super thanky.

Love, Dad

Letter 3

Admiration vs. *Popularity*

Everybody's private motto: It's better to be popular than right.

Mark Twain

Do not yearn to be popular; be exquisite.

Do not desire to be famous; be loved.

C.Joybell C.

My shining offspring,

If you look at my high school senior yearbook, you will discover that I was runner-up in the category: Best Personality. Runner-up. Great. So, I had the *second-best* personality, behind Gary Deaton.

There was no actual contest. Gary and I didn't deliver a campaign speech to the entire school. He was a big, likable, not-very-talkative fellow. I could've wiped the stage with him in wit, buoyancy and charm. He was a football player, a guard. He could have physically wiped the stage with me. So, it was just a popularity vote, right? Everybody went to the football games. Everybody watched Gary and the Bulldogs make touchdowns. I, on the other hand, for reasons of stature and self-preservation (a self-reliant, skinny wimp) was on the golf team. Nobody got to witness my occasional brilliant shot (OK, very occasional), my eloquent commentary (creative cussing) and lighting fast swing on the links. (Note: a lightning-fast swing is good in baseball, but not golf. My nickname was 'the Whip'.) So, clearly, Gary's visibility gave him an unfair advantage.

That was many years ago, but my offer still stands to serve in his place if Gary should be unable to carry out the duties of "Best Personality."

In the yearbook there were other awards: Most Handsome and Most Beautiful; Friendliest; Most Likely to Succeed; Best School Spirit and Senior Favorites. But there were no categories for Most Admired or Kindest or Best Character. The honor that came closest was the award for Service. Phil Dietz won that. I still admire him. His award was prophetic. Phil has lived a life of service in Christian ministry and mission work.

I wonder who in my high school graduating class would have won Most Admired? Kindest? or Best Character? Certainly not me. Not even runner-up to the runner-up.

No doubt about it, it feels good to be liked. It feels even better to be liked by a lot of people. Being liked is not a bad thing unless you get hooked on it. You can count on this: if you take a strong stand for something, you are likely to be very unpopular with a lot of people.

> "I don't know of a quicker way to become unpopular
> than to disagree."
>
> John Brunner - author

Being liked is a powerful motive. These days people in our personal social internet can click a button and "like" us, or what we say or do. Talent shows are driven by millions of people voting for their "Favorite." But simply getting more people to vote for you or get them in your corner emotionally can give you a false sense of value and reality. What if they stop liking you? Or actually "unfriend" you? What if they don't vote for you? What if they stop lapping up what you're selling? Where are you then? Who are you then?

> Fame is a bee.
> It has a song -
> It has a sting -
> Ah, too, it has a wing
>
> Emily Dickinson – poet

My dears, popularity can make us depend more on what people think of us, than on what we think of ourselves. Even more, it can outweigh what God himself thinks of us.

> If God in all his infinite power and love were real to us,
> the opinions of men, either for or against us…
> would shrink into nothingness by comparison.
>
> Dave Hunt – author

So, what does God think of us? For too many people, "God loves you" has become a religious cliché that has lost its power. But he does - to the point of painful sacrifice. He is also in our corner. "If God is for us who can be against us?" (Romans 8:31). And there is also this, and it's one of my favorites because it plainly says how God feels about us. Psalm 18 verse 19 says, "He rescued me because he delighted in me." Is that awesome? Or what? That should satisfy better than anything popularity can deliver. And I can relate to it, because as a father, your father, of course, I love you. But I also delight in you. I am crazy about you!

So apparently, we are very popular with God Almighty. And yet, we have this human itch to be popular with people. We can pay more attention to that itch than the deep hunger for love, satisfied primarily by God himself. We are so human. And that's understandable. But wacky and conflicted.

> We are so vain that we care for the opinion of
> those we don't care for.
>
> Marie Von Ebner-Eschenbach – novelist

My dear young humans, the itch to be liked, or popular, is a common insecurity. Scratch it and it spreads like poison ivy. Its driving force is fear. By contrast, the desire to be admired goes deeper than an itch. It's a core hunger. Feed it and it will humble and satisfy you. Its driving force is significance. (See the letter: Success vs. Significance)

Popularity says, "You are cool or attractive or rich, therefore you are somebody." Until you do something uncool, lose your looks or money. Admiration says, "You are somebody because God made you and delights in you, therefore, you are cool and attractive and rich in a way that really matters."

To show you what I mean, let me tell you briefly about a princess and a nun.

* * *

Once upon a time in England (long ago in the 1980's), a young, beautiful woman named Diana became a princess. Before that, no one really knew who she was. She was from a noble family line but not from royalty. She lived quietly, working with children at a daycare center. No claim to fame. All that changed when a Prince married her, not for love but by obligation to the crown. So, she became Diana, Princess of Wales. Their wedding was one of the most viewed events of the twentieth century.

Princess Diana gained great popularity everywhere, mainly for her beauty, royal status, gracious manner and later, her compassion. She and the Prince had two sons and all the riches the world can offer, but after some years the loveless marriage ended in divorce. Diana lost her royal status and became known simply as "Di." She remained very popular as a gentle, perhaps a little sad, intriguing figure who went about doing good. (She supported more than a hundred charities.)

Meanwhile, on the other side of the world, in a place where suffering and poverty are a way of life, a nun named Teresa worked tirelessly and unnoticed with lepers and the poor. After several decades, word of her great compassion and love for the sick and dying spread around the world. Many people traveled to the slums of Calcutta, India, to discover the power and wisdom of "Mother" Theresa, as she came to be known. Eventually, presidents and world leaders invited her to speak in the halls of government and great universities. The admiration she inspired made her very popular. Mother Teresa even won a Nobel Peace Prize. On the other hand, her uncompromising Christian views made her unpopular with many "moderns." But even they admired her.

The nun and the princess both achieved world-wide visibility by very different roads. In fact, their paths actually crossed several times. They met briefly for a third time in New York City in June 1997. What a picture that was - the famous princess and the simple servant nun.

Sadly, one night in Paris, just six weeks after their last meeting, Diana was killed in a violent car crash while being chased at high speed by photographers. A shocked world grieved. I did, too. She was only forty-four. Just when Di's popularity as a celebrity began to shift to true admiration because of her compassion and the noble causes she supported, popularity actually killed her. One million people lined the streets of London to catch a glimpse of the funeral procession. Two and a half billion viewed around the world, nearly half the population of the planet! A pop star sang a hit song about her.

Five days later, twenty-four hours before Diana's funeral, Mother Theresa died from a heart attack in Calcutta. She was eighty-seven. The coverage of Di's death nearly pushed Mother Theresa's death out of the media. Thousands viewed her body for a week and fifteen thousand filled a stadium for the ceremony. A few hymns were sung. No pop star sang a hit song about her.

Apparently, more people will turn out to see a princess than a saint. As Holden Caulfield said, "People always clap for the wrong things." (from JD Salinger's "The Catcher in the Rye." More on that in the letter: Significance vs. Success.)

* * *

Just so you know, Runner-up for Best Personality is not the only award I have ever received. I've been given a few others: Best Cast, for a fishing skill competition in Boy Scouts. First Place for my age group in Punt-Pass & Kick. Being scrawny, I couldn't get much distance, but my accuracy made my points add up to more than the bigger boys. I've received Frequent Flyer awards for mileage flown (or is that re-wards?). I have also won a few awards for songs I've written.

These do not compare to the best award I've ever received. God awarded me - you. That's right. He awarded me, you, like living trophies of his mercy on me. I have no idea why he would consider me for such an honor. Maybe he wanted me to experience the kind of love and delight that he knows as a father. If so, that part of His plan has worked. But I not only love you and delight in you. I admire you, who you are, and who you are becoming. So, by far, the award I treasure more than any other, the one that isn't stored in a box or sits on a shelf collecting dust, the one I carry with me every day, is this: Most Blessed Dad.

My dear growing-up-too-fast little ones, all along the way you will come to places where two roads diverge into the world. One will appeal to an itch to stand out, be noticed. The other will call deeper to your spirit. Down one road, the applause of the crowd and your peers will be a strong drug. Down the other road lies deep inner satisfaction and the applause of heaven, which for now is more distant but far sweeter. Thank you for always pointing me down the sweeter road.

Love, Dad

Letter 4

Courage vs. *Bravado*

Any fool knows that bravado is always a cover-up for insecurity.

Bobby Darin (singer)

Real courage is when you know you're licked before you begin but you begin anyway, and you see it through no matter what.

Atticus Finch
from To Kill a Mockingbird

My brave hearts,

Bravado sounds like "brave" doesn't it? "Courage" nearly sounds like "corsage," but one is just a small bunch of flowers pinned to a woman's dress that will soon wither and die. The other, courage, is something else entirely.

Here's an easy example. A kid blurts to another kid on the playground, "I bet my dad can beat up your dad." Clearly bravado, right? There is not much to lose by making that statement. Nothing at stake for the kid spewing it. There is no real risk, except for the dads, if it should come to blows.

Compare that to this: "I bet my God can beat up your God." Sounds like bravado, right? But what if it was backed up by a contest to see whose God really has power? That's basically what the biblical prophet Elijah said and did to the prophets of Baal who agreed to a contest. Elijah waited and watched as the followers of Baal danced and shouted all day and even cut their own flesh, pleading for Baal to show up and light the altar on fire. Pretty good dramatics. But Baal was a no-show. No fire. Nothing happened. Elijah stepped up. For good measure, he soaked the whole altar with water. Three times! Then he called on the God of Jacob, Isaac and Israel. Immediately, fire came from the sky, burned up the altar and the offering on it! That is courage. Something was at stake. There was actual risk involved. Not just jaw-flapping.

Bravado is everywhere these days. It's especially easy to spot on the bumper of the car in front of us. A lot of people feel bold enough to say on their bumper what they would probably never say aloud to your face. "Eat the rich!" "Impeach the President" "Darwin's missing link = FAITH" "If we're supposed to be vegetarians then why are cows made of meat?" (Ok, that's just plain funny.)

How about this bumper sticker I actually spotted on a car? "Just Say No to Christ" Here in the USA, a country that protects free speech, it's pretty easy to pick on the gracious, death-defying carpenter God and his turn-the-other-cheek followers. Not much risk there unless you're afraid of getting prayed for. I wonder if the person driving that bumper sticker around would display, "Just say no to Allah." Would that be bravado or take a bit of courage? How about displaying that on your car if you live next to a mosque or in some Middle Eastern country? Courageous? Or just plain dumb?

Bravado is putting a bumper sticker on your car. Courage is not only speaking but living the truth, face-to-face, day-to-day, even against opposition, sometimes facing actual danger, in the real world.

Take the Declaration of Independence. Was it just fancy jaw flapping by the founding fathers? "When in the course of human events it becomes necessary for one people to dissolve the political bands which have connected them with another... We hold these truths to be self-evident," etc. Was that document just an eloquent bluff thinking it wouldn't come to war with King George? Hardly. It stands as one of the most courageous statements in history. But it wasn't merely a statement. It was an act, signed in ink but established with blood.

* * *

Let me give you a picture of courage closer to home. You have heard me tell this story, but let me write it down for you.

One summer day, July 24, 1968, my little brother, Brad, did not look in the mirror that morning and say to the sixty-eight-pound reflection looking back, "Today I'm going to be courageous." But that's what July 24, 1968, held in store for your future uncle.

Later that day, just after midnight on a calm, clear West Texas night, he and my dad were preparing to steer the boat back onto the waiting trailer after fishing. The boat glided across the glassy inlet. At just the right moment, Dad goosed the throttle sending the boat squeaking and groaning onto the trailer. He cut the engine. My other brother, Barry, shifted the station wagon into gear and hauled them out a few feet. Before anyone could move to complete the familiar tie-down routine, a car came barreling down the broad boat ramp. Like a stampeding buffalo with headlights, it plunged into the water, bobbed fifty feet from shore and began to sink. Before dad could get the d of "don't" out of his mouth, Brad was in the water and swimming toward the car. Dad and Barry immediately relaunched the boat.

In such moments, reality stretches time at the seams. Somewhere between unreal slow motion and thundering heartbeats, Brad reached the car. It pitched forward and down from the weight of the engine, the headlights creating two murky ghosts. Water cascaded through the open windows and my skinny little brother pulled ("floated" he says) a woman from the open driver side window. As Dad maneuvered the boat close enough for him and Barry to get them on board, Lake Meredith lapped up and over the roof of the car.

Apparently unfamiliar with the area, the twenty-five-year-old driver mistook the newly constructed ramp for a highway. She was lost but making good time. Soggy and shaken, she was alive… because of my little brother, your uncle.

The next spring, thirteen-year-old Tenderfoot Scout, Thomas Bradley Sprague, received the highest award in the Boy Scouts and was flown across the Lone Star state to be honored at a banquet. Today, the Honor Medal hangs in the hallway near his own children's bedrooms, framed with the newspaper clipping and picture of him in his scout uniform. Our family remembers proudly. Wherever she is today, I bet that lady remembers, too.

I wasn't on the fishing trip that night, but being the eldest of three brothers, I have no doubt I would have beaten Brad into the water. Ok, I have *some* doubt. What would I have done?

Most people probably wonder how they will react in crisis situations. Would we risk our lives? Jump in the water? Dive in front of a car to push someone out of danger? Would we take a bullet for someone? We don't really know until faced with the crisis. Anyone can talk big. But who will walk big when it counts? Bravado talks. Courage walks. Sometimes leaps. That night at a lake in West Texas, there was no time to theorize or think at all.

Is there courage inside each of us, waiting only for the moment of testing to be revealed?

Shakespeare said, "Some are born great, some achieve greatness, and some have greatness thrust upon them." Jesus told his disciples, "Greater love has no one than this, that he lay down his life for his friends,." Understandably, we tend to measure greatness and courage by extreme and dramatic acts of selflessness, risk, and achievement. But don't the words of Jesus and a nearly universal longing for noble purpose point to this: that all, not some of us, are born with the potential for greatness, for courage?

A troubled teenager expressed so well the hunger most of us have for some measure of greatness, purpose and courage. He confided to his therapist a vision of what he would really like to do with his life. He said:

> I keep picturing all these kids playing some game in this
> big field of rye and all. Thousands of little kids, and
> nobody's around – nobody big, I mean – except me.
> And I'm standing on the edge of some crazy cliff. What
> I have to do, I have to catch everybody if they start to go
> over the cliff – I mean if they're running and they don't
> look where they're going I have to come out from
> somewhere and catch them. That's all I'd do all day. I'd

just be the catcher in the rye and all. I know it's crazy, but that's the only thing I'd really like to be.

That is Holden Caulfield, from J. D. Salinger's classic, *Catcher in the Rye*. (You gotta read it.) He is a fictional character speaking real-life matters of the heart. Holden longed for a life worth living, or to use a currently popular term, a purpose-driven life.

Your Uncle Brad was a Catcher in the Right Place and Time, so to speak, at least for one person. Was he born for that one event on that summer day? Probably not, but he certainly proved courageous when a moment of greatness was thrust upon him. And he did one thing that is within your reach, everyone's reach, something that Shakespeare left out.

If I may cross pens with that other William, the great Shakespeare, I think his famous statement missed one essential element of greatness and courage: Choosing it. Your uncle Brad chose. Greatness or courage is most often the result of choices, not just one dramatic choice in a moment of urgency - but a series of choices – about values, identity, principles and purpose. And those choices build up, one at a time, and combine to make us who we are. The person who avoids those choices, or chooses unwisely, also becomes the sum of their poor choices. Most people, you and I included, make some good choices and some poor choices. It's never too soon to start making the good ones.

History is full of stories about ordinary people who did extraordinary things, people who were kids at one time, just like you, who made choices and faced challenges that shaped them into courageous people. Sadly, there is also no shortage of jaw flappers who talk big but walk small. You will run into both kinds - on the playground, at school, on the highway, in the movies, on TV and down the years - at work, where you live and play, and especially in politics. Learn to spot the difference now. (See the letter: Politician vs. Leader)

* * *

Here's the sum of it. Bravado is very much like a corsage of words that withers and dies, but courage is a true strength of heart that stands the test of trial and time and blossoms again with every remembrance of it. Bravado fades. Courage endures. It can plant itself in the hearts of many people, even future generations, and inspire again and again, like Elijah's contest or the Declaration of Independence or your uncle Brad's heroism.

My brave young hearts, there is a saying: I'd rather see a sermon than hear one. When you get old enough to drive and own your own cars, you can put any message you want on your bumper. It's a free country. But I would rather your bumpers be blank, and your lives speak volumes. I am so thankful that your shiny, young hearts are already a treasure trove to me - of courage in the making.

Ice Cream vs. *Frozen Yogurt*

Men often applaud an imitation and hiss the real thing.

Aesop – ancient Greek storyteller

My sweets,

Ok, if you don't get this one I'm truly concerned about your ability to navigate the subtle shell games of a crafty world.

You know how much I love ice cream, especially homemade. My collection of eighty ice cream scoops on the kitchen wall bears testimony to that. I once thought of opening an ice cream shop called "Paradise Frost." Didn't. But I still own the domain name.

Having nurtured you on quality ice cream in your early years, especially my own homemade creations, I have faith that you already have the scoop on this one. But let me make my case anyway.

Frozen yogurt, while semi-satisfying on a hot summer day, was created by the same clever, well-meaning but market-driven people who brought us diet drinks, skim milk (white water), non-dairy coffee creamers (no cows involved), and low-fat graham crackers made from recycled cardboard (or at least taste like cardboard).

For full disclosure, I have often settled for frozen yogurt in an airport or mall, but I cannot remember a single experience being

28

fully satisfying, especially considering the high price of such a letdown.

Granted, the main ingredients in yogurt and ice cream are similar, milk and milk products, but the similarity and savor end there.

First, the word "yogurt" itself - come on? It's like the name of a cute, dumb cartoon character, or the sound of someone barfing. I'm not saying yummy treat is sinister. But the playful name masks a devious side. So, let the buyer beware and know the real truth.

"Yogurt" is actually a Turkish word that means "to knead" or mix together. That is exactly what the creators of frozen yogurt did. They mixed a bunch of stuff together - stabilizers, like animal and vegetable gelatins, caseinate derivatives like citrates, phosphates, emulsifiers like fatty acids, mineral salts, *artificial* colors and *artificial* sweeteners with names like Acesulfame K, Maltitol and Aspertame. (Don't those sound like the names of alien invaders on Star Trek?) One of the main flavor agents in frozen yogurt actually includes an inoculation of bacteria! That's right. *Lactobacillus bulgaricus* and *Streptococcus thermophilous* are included in the mixture to create a certain flavor. Does that sound like things found in a kitchen? or a laboratory?

On top of all that, two of the biggest ingredients in frozen yogurt are… are you ready? Water and air! Talk about Shinola.

I guess you can't make a very good living asking people to step up and pay for a serving of Lactobacillus, tiny ice crystals, air and chemicals. So, you gotta find a cute, exotic name. "Frozen Shinola" would have been accurate, but too honest. Pile O'Crappola was already taken to describe most political speeches, so someone landed on - Yogurt.

Now, let me ask you a question. Often, the right question will point you in the direction of the sacred. Would you prefer (A) to eat in a laboratory serving up a concoction "cooked up" by a chemist and marketing guru, or (B) in a colorful shop or at home where rich, smooth ice cream is prepared by a chef or dad from natural ingredients all found in a grocery store?

I rest my case. And trust your judgment.

By the way, Bill Murray, the comedian and actor, said the best way to teach your children about taxes is to "eat thirty percent of their ice cream." Not their yogurt.

My savor seekers, let me remind you that even the best ice cream or best of anything this planet has to offer are only hints of the truly sacred. It's no stretch to imagine the mountains of heaven capped with a paradise frost tastier than anything in the rich buffet of this world. Tasting it there together will be one of the sweetest things ever.

Love, Dad

Letter 6

Reading vs. *Screen Time*

"So, please, oh PLEASE, we beg, we pray,
Go throw your TV set away,
And in its place you can install,
A lovely bookshelf on the wall."

Roald Dahl
from Charlie and the Chocolate Factory

My talented troupe,

One of the major regrets of my life is that I do not play piano. Every time I walk by one in someone's home, a hotel lobby or a recording studio, something in me sinks. I cannot sit down and simply play a song. Dangnatious.

What did I do with all those hours as a kid, outside of school? A lot of things: built forts, model airplanes and ships, homework, chores, Cub Scouts, Boy Scouts, played baseball and golf, goofed off, cruised on my bike, hung around and read comic books - but not *real* books. My love for reading and books didn't come till much later. But piano lessons never came at all.

When it comes to advice about reading, I have to come clean. I only finished one book at Stephen F. Austin Junior High and one in high school. *Pilot Down Presumed Dead*, a survival story about a small plane going down on an island. (What kept me reading it was... nope... read it yourself;) In high school, *A Tale of Two Cities* hooked me. Wyatt, so far, that's your favorite book. Ms. Arthur, English teacher my junior year, enticed us to keep plowing through it. I remember my resistance turning to curiosity. The pace picked up as I wondered what was going to happen to the main character, Charles Darnay. I actually started to care what happened to him. And then the ending – Bam! How could words on a page have such an effect on me? The ending almost made me cry, but back then high school boys in Texas didn't cry much, especially over a book. (You see, what Charles Darnay did was... nope... read it yourself;)

That experience with Charles Dickens began my awakening to the power of reading and the written word, and helped steer me to major in literature in college. Later, as you know, I even started to write books. Now here I sit, hoping to find the words to stir something in you.

I am so glad you've already surpassed my childhood reading list, which didn't take much. I would rather see your face in a book than on a screen. These days you've got it even harder. The screen is right in your hand - with you everywhere you go.

Ever wonder why your mom and I limited your time on electronic gadgetry? It's part of our job to keep the Shinola time bandits from stealing your precious hours and affections.

I have to confess, in my early years my eyes and brain were chained to television. That hypnotic moving picture box was invented a few years before I was born. It took the world by storm. Families gathered around it, mesmerized by the soft light of images and voices streaming from somewhere beyond our own world and experience.

More recently, on a trip to Mali, Africa, I witnessed this in a small village of round mud huts with straw roofs. Some huts actually had TV antennas! Electricity only ran for two hours in the evening. Just after sundown, small TV sets appeared just outside the front doors. Families huddled around to watch some local programming mixed with reruns of American shows like "I Love Lucy." Apparently, the power of those dancing light boxes is hard to resist worldwide.

Television cast its spell over me early on with kid shows like Captain Kangaroo, Huckleberry Hound, Superman, and a local cartoon show hosted by an interplanetary traveler, Major Komar. He said a magic word that would start every cartoon, "Eeeny-Gawana-Geeny". My brothers and sisters and I said it together, watching on our den floor, "Eeeny-Gawana-Geeny," and we felt the power. My Cub Scout troop got to visit Major Komar's show at the television station in Amarillo. We even sat in his spaceship. How many earthlings can say that?

The years that followed were held hostage by Saturday morning cartoons, afternoon comedies like Gilligan's Island. I know this is going to sound like the 1800s, but we only had three channels to choose from! Three! Sundays we watched NFL football and were devoted followers the great wizard himself on Walt Disney Presents.

I have a bedtime memory of my dad getting to stay up later than us to watch the 9:00 p.m. variety shows, followed by the ten o'clock news. He dunked Oreos in a glass of milk, while I had to go off to bed and listen to the muffled music, laughter, and commercials through the walls. I remember thinking, "Ah, so, that's what true freedom and adulthood look like. When I grow up I'm gonna stay up late, watch TV and snack." Impressive goals, huh?

It pains me to think how many hours of my life I sacrificed to that glowing box. There is no telling how many instruments I could play by now if, instead of watching television, I had spent that time practicing. Not to mention the benefit to my mind and soul. So, for your consideration, my lesson learned motivated me to limit your screen time in the hope that you squander fewer hours of your childhood than I did.

> I find television very educating. Every time somebody
> turns on the set, I go into the other room and read a book.
>
> Groucho Marx

Television, like many things, can be used for good or far less than good. It's a powerful tool for the master storyteller. But it's also one of the Shinola peddler's greatest allies. Even the few things worth watching are selling something - a viewpoint, a value system and, of course, stuff. On one level, this is simply the way the world works. Most people have to work to make a living. So, everyone is selling. Television and all screen services excel in a key strategy of Shinola peddling. They use shiny, attractive things, stories, humor, hype and emotion to do one thing – create desire – to make us want what we do not have. It's called "desire marketing."

Marketers, in general, aim to make us want something, say, a "shiny new bike" or a space age breakfast drink that "actual astronauts drink!" A doll that actually cries and wets its diaper! How can any little girl live without that? The list never stops growing. The "most realistic" video game ever. A "fresh and improved" detergent or shampoo. A "bigger better, tastier" burger. A "once in a lifetime" offer. A new "smarter" car. They offer us the "safest" tire on the road. A "sale of the century." A "revolutionary" diet that includes a remarkable new treat called "frozen yogurt." (See the letter: Ice Cream vs. Frozen Yogurt)

You see, the creators of programming make their money by attracting an audience to sell things for their sponsors or advertisers. They offer great stuff and thrilling experiences we can't possibly live without. How about a dream vacation? A full head of hair? (No jokes, please) And they will present whatever it takes to keep us glued to the screen until the next commercial. Make us laugh. Make us cry. Make us want. Make us buy. And now the buy button is on our phones and almost always in our hands.

In order to break the screen's hypnotic hold on you, and at the risk of you being temporarily irritated with your mom and me, summer reading lists, piano, drum, dance, soccer and other activities are partly for your benefit and partly for my atonement. Music lessons are not intended to shape you into a world class musician, but to fill some of your hours and your spirit with something more fortifying than being led passively away by the Pied Pipers on the screen who never sleep.

Now, many years since my childhood, much of what's on television and screens reflects and sells a world extremely eroded from what is true and sacred. As your father, it seems even more urgent for me to direct you elsewhere to feed and shape your soul - often by simply hitting the "off" button for you. "Carpe Remoto!" That's corrupted Latin for "seize the remote." When you want to veg, grab another cookie and are not willing or able to break the magnetic beam from the screen that holds you in its glimmering grip, I can break the spell – with the push of a button. You're welcome.

Except for some occasionally fine storytelling, inspiring nature and history shows, some good laughs and being aware of the world at large, there is very little on screens worth the cost of even one or two hours of a day of your life. Certainly, there is precious little to lead you to a sacred moment or revelation you cannot find elsewhere. Why wade through the tantalizing tactics of high tech Shinola and dumb shows to discover a crumb of food for your soul? I'm amazed there is still an "off" button on the remote. Maybe that's coming soon. But not to our home. Once again, you're welcome.

Besides stealing productive things like reading time, there is another theft committed by Shinola merchants trying to keep your finger away from the off button.

Ben Franklin, a wise and innovative founder of our nation, said, "Early to bed and early to rise makes a man healthy, wealthy and wise." Apparently, it also makes for more intelligent children.

> …amongst children of preschool age, the more
> intelligent ones tend to sleep less than the dull ones.
> After the age of seven this relationship is reversed, the
> more intelligent school children sleeping more than
> the dull ones.
>
> Desmond Morris, The Naked Ape 1967

Imagine that. Intelligent children sleep more. Smarter people tend to make wiser choices. (Though not always. See the letter: Wisdom vs. Education.) Shinola peddlers know that dumb, well, less thoughtful people might be a kinder way to put that, make more gullible customers, easier prey for the pitchman or politician. (See the letter: Leader vs. Politician) So, wise parents send their children to bed – with a bedtime story from a favorite book. You're welcome. (And don't forget to brush your teeth.)

Here's another impact from an obsession with TV, and now the little screen in your hands:

> "Rich people have small TVs and big libraries,
> and poor people have small libraries and big TVs."

> Zig Ziglar – author

That's right, the more hours of life we spend watching a screen, the less productive we are. (Except perhaps for those who make their living on a computer screen, like writers, of course.) Instead of a constant barrage of input from the Pied Pipers of programming, imagine having some ideas and thoughts of your own, ideas that lead to significance and perhaps financial benefit and stability.

For full disclosure, until you came along I led a very non-Ben-Franklin, fairly late-to-bed, not so early-to-rise life. Being a musician and single for a long time before I met your mother, I was a night owl. As time went by, I began to use those hours to read great books or write something instead of vegging in front of a screen. Even now I have to fight the urge to hook up to the electronic feeding tube of 24-hour news and entertainment, and simply go to bed in order to be more fit for the next day. As another William put it:

Sleep… knits up the raveled sleeve of care.
William Shakespeare - Macbeth II, 2,37

I have to thank you, my dear children, for the part you played in helping me rediscover the glory of early morning. I first discovered it on fishing trips with my dad, heading out before sunrise to catch a few sacred moments. Some of the richest (and sleepiest) moments of my life have been coming into your rooms to find one of you reaching up to me for that first cozy hug of the new day. How exquisite. And how fleeting those times (dang-alluia). The finest, softest, most expensive blanket in the world cannot compare to your little arms around my neck and your warm cheek next to mine as the sun rose.

I never met an early riser who was a late bloomer. So, any time you have the option to read a good book, play piano, drums or guitar, draw a picture, write a letter or poem – or stay up and watch television or scroll a screen – redeem the day by doing any of the former - or just go to bed. Why invite a parade of mostly Shinola peddlers to steal away your life?

Of course, there are a few good reasons to stay up past bedtime: an Andy Griffith rerun, especially with Barney Fife in it; a good movie and popcorn with mom or dad; or a child out past curfew. In that case, sleep for a parent is rarely an option.

All the days meant for me were written in Your book
before one of them came to be. Psalm 139:16

So, my bedtime negotiators and daydreamers, Carpe Diem. That's
actually good Latin for "Seize the day." Make the most of your
childhood days. They are precious, numbered and counting down.
I am here to help you make more of them than I did, and am
happy to say you are well on your way.

Someday, when you walk by a piano or guitar or drum, sit down
and send beautiful notes into the air – or get lost reading a story
you can't put down... you're welcome.

Love, Dad

Letter 7

Significance vs. *Success*

It is not the things we get, but the hearts we touch
that will measure our success in life.

Charlie Brown

What good would it be for someone to gain the whole world,
yet lose their soul?

Jesus - Matthew 16:26

My emerging masterpieces,

Christmas 1982, my dad gave me a gift that sits on the mantle
to this day. It's a wall plaque, only six inches by eight. You've seen
it. On it is a simple scene, misty blue, probably just before sunrise,
of a father and son fishing from the end of a dock. The son, about
ten-years old, stands looking down at his father, who appears to
be telling him something. I grew up fishing with my dad. Those
times are still my favorite memories of him. So, the picture alone
speaks volumes. But what made this one of the most fortifying
things dad ever did for me is the quote in the lower right corner.

Try not to become a man of success but rather a man of value.

Albert Einstein

Your Grandpa was always a man of few words. One of the first
of the few letters I ever got from him, he wrote on a prescription

40

pad probably while standing behind the counter at his pharmacy. It contained four sentences and only eleven words. It arrived during my first semester at college.

> Son,
> Study hard.
> Sleep some.
> Cut hair.
> Need money?
> Love, Dad.

That was in the early 70s when long hair for young men equaled a manifesto of freedom. Songs were even written about it. "Almost Cut My Hair" by Crosby, Stills, Nash & Young proclaimed the glory of letting your "freak flag fly."

Early on, Dad fought the hair rebellion and my first trip home from college at Thanksgiving became a battleground. I arrived Wednesday afternoon like a headline: Firstborn Son Returns Victorious From College. I was excited to see my family and had a new college buddy with me. Ken Brown. He was much more colorful than his monochrome name. He was a short, pale, droopy art major in an oversized khaki flak jacket. Ken wore owl-eyed, John Lennon glasses, surrounded by a curly mop of long hair in a loose afro accompanied by a bit of a whine in his voice. My hair was tame by comparison - not even as long as the Beatles' mop top haircuts in 1964. Get the picture? We came through the door like returning conquerors. Loud hellos and hugs from mom and siblings erupted in the kitchen. I turned into the living room to set down my bag. Dad entered from the far end of the room. He just looked at me. There was no open-arm welcome. All he said was, "Damn, look at your hair."

The next morning, on Thanksgiving day, Dad woke me up early. We drove to a barber shop. In our small town he knew a barber who would accommodate us. We rode in silence. Ken, incredulous, rode in the back seat, Dad and I in the front. Not a word was spoken. And I got my hair cut.

Years later, we laughed about that episode. Dad expressed how bad he felt about that. But it became part of the backdrop that made his gift of the wall plaque at Christmas 1982 so monumental. I think he would agree, hair style has nothing to do with being a man of value.

* * *

Throughout my years of college and graduate school, interrupted by two years of playing music in a band on the road, Dad encouraged me more than a few times to take a couple of business classes so I would know how that part of the world works. He knew how hard it is to make a living and raise a family of five kids. I showed little interest in his advice, insisting there just wasn't room in my literature curriculum, which included three rounds of English Romantic Poets. Naturally, he was concerned about how I would be successful at making a living, especially as I headed to Nashville to pursue music full time.

Some years later, the first time I applied for a mortgage, I realized how wise a father can be. And how dense a son. The ability to quote Keats carries no weight with a loan officer quoting interest rates and points and escrow and closing costs on adjustable and fixed loans. (How much does a Grecian urn anyway? Never mind. You get the point.)

That real world wake up made Dad's gift of Christmas '82 even more monumental. It continues to remind me of his true heart toward me. And now it is mine toward you. He wanted me to be able to make my way in the world, financially and career wise, but his gift spoke of a higher value. Dad affirmed me with just the right words and gift. He gave me a compass heading toward what mattered most. And now I pass that compass heading along to you.

We all have to work at something, trade our time and talent for treasure to pay the bills. I could write you a separate letter, Calling vs. Career, but that idea fits here.

The best of both is to make a living by doing something significant, something you love, something directly related to your gifting or God-given wiring. That's what can make a job more than a career, something tied to your destiny.

I worked a lot of different jobs when I was young. A paper route. I delivered donuts. Worked at a golf course restocking soda and beer in the coolers, filling the ball washers around the course. One summer, I worked in the back of a dry cleaner. Was it hot? In a Texas summer? No, it was damn hot. But the dry-cleaning job had a significance. My dad wanted me to help the owner, Ed Cartwright, whose surgery prevented him from lifting anything. I learned a lot from Mr. Cartwright about removing stains, but a lot more from the kind way he treated people. And me.

Later, in college, I painted houses, stocked books at a bookstore, worked in a warehouse filling two-gallon plastic bottles with cleaning fluids from fifty-five-gallon drums. I mentioned before that I took two years off school to play music in a band at Disneyland and Disneyworld, did a USO tour and a string of nightclubs. None of those were "callings." In graduate school, I sensed a hint of a calling to teach English, but another fork in the road led elsewhere.

In all the searching for "what do I want to be when I grow up" there are turning points in life. God has a hand in the choreography of these. Watch for them.

One Spring when I was working as a carpenter in Denton, Texas, a friend, Cindy, sat me down and read me the Parable of the Talents that Jesus told. It's recorded in Matthew 25. Read it for yourself, but here's the gist. A wealthy man leaving on a journey puts three employees in charge of three different amounts of talents, "each according to his ability." A talent was worth about twenty years' wages! So, it was a lot of money. To one, he entrusted five talents. Let's say about $50,000 back then. To another, two talents, $20,000. And one talent to a third employee, $10,000. The first two doubled the money. The third dug a hole and buried it. He was afraid to lose it and have nothing to show the owner. After a long time, the man returned to settle accounts. He put the first two employees in charge of even bigger things. As you might expect, the owner was beyond displeased with the fearful employee. He took his $10K, split it between the other two and threw the lazy employee out, where there was "darkness and gnashing of teeth." Not pleasant, to say the least.

Cindy applied a velvet crowbar, urging me to do something

with the musical gifts entrusted to me or when God settled accounts, he would be "hacked." A few weeks later, her brother, Michael, invited me to Nashville to become part of a new music venture. That door opened to my calling and career.

No matter how much ability we have, God expects us to use it. On the way to finding your calling and career, you will work some jobs that are clearly not tied to your destiny or gifting. It doesn't matter if you serve chicken sandwiches, stock groceries at a store, deliver furniture from a warehouse, wait tables or make a living carving golf tees out of fallen giant redwoods. You can be a person of value in all those settings.

More than becoming successful as the world defines it, I want you to discover the joy of making a difference, of being part of something bigger than you. Whatever you choose to do in this life, I hope you excel at it and enjoy it. But I pray that making a difference is actually more fun and energizing for you than making dollars and cents (See Letter 23: God vs. Gold), and more rewarding than hearing applause or receiving awards or promotions. There is nothing better than the sound of "Well done" from a dad who beams not because of what you have accomplished but because of who you have become. And even greater will be the "Well done" from our Heavenly Father.

This can sound like a monumental endeavor. But living a life that matters doesn't have to be a grandiose thing, like finding a cure for cancer or rallying the entire world around a noble cause. The finest life, like the finest painting, is created one brush stroke at a time. Every day, simply determine to do one significant thing. This will often involve doing something for someone else. Call your mom or a friend. Leave a generous tip at a restaurant. Pay the bill for the person in the car behind you at a drive-through. Donate to a need or volunteer to help after a calamity. Anonymously pay someone's electric or medical bill. Play with a child. Or sit with and read to a friend who is grieving.

A friend did that for me once. Ken left his job, wife and kids at home, got on a plane to Nashville to spend a few days with me in a dark time. During that same painful season, another friend, Ed, slept on the floor by my bed, so when I woke up in hollow shock or tears someone would be there. Talk about significant. That was it, and not just for me, but for them, too.

Most of the time, significance will come very simply. Call your mom. Did I mention that already? Ok. Then call your Dad. Read a good book, especially the Bible (See the letter: Awe vs. Wow)

I quoted this before, but it bears repeating here. Psalm 139 verse 16 says, "All the days ordained for me were written in your book before one of them came to be." Every day that passes means one less ahead of us. Make them count so that your days and your life, do not evaporate into a blur of activity instead of action, or consist of mere motion rather than movement toward a higher, deeper life.

My flesh and blood works of art, every day can be a brush stroke in the masterpiece of your life, which I have to say, already adds such bright colors to mine.

Letter 8

Virtue vs. *Beauty*

You can fake virtue for an audience.
You can't fake it in your own eyes.

Ayn Rand

Beauty is fleeting.
Solomon - Proverbs 31:30

My virtuosos,

Willow, do you remember this? We were all in the car on our way home from one of your brother's soccer games. A hit song from that time came on the radio. As usual, you were singing beautiful harmony to it. The song is about seeing a guy for the first time, being completely knocked out by him and his "ripped jeans, skin was showin." Apparently, he's so drop-dead handsome the singer can hardly look at him. But she says, "Hey, I just met you and this is crazy, but here's my number. Call me maybe." (*Call Me Maybe* by Carly Rae Jepsen)

Doing my dad thing, I told you I wanted you to find a man with a drop-dead heart. I joked about writing a song for you to sing called, "I'm Lookin for a Drop-Dead Heart." Without skipping a beat, you responded, "I know, Dad, of course. But can he be a hunk, too?"

Good one, dear daughter. Of course. There are good men out there who are also hunks. (You're thinking, me, right?)

My sons, as men, we're not immune to the lure of outward beauty either. In fact, historically, we have a pretty predictable track record of falling for a pretty face over a drop-dead heart. I've been there. Done that. Just look at all the "beautiful" people who get together, but don't last very long.

King David comes to mind. His lapse of virtue with Bathsheba began by watching her take a bath on her rooftop near his palace. (Hmm. Did she have no other options? Hey, is this crazy? I take a bath, you can watch, call me maybe.) The prophet Samuel described her as "very beautiful." She was married. He was married. He was the King, and still a hunk at nearly fifty years old. Her husband was away fighting a war. For David. She didn't need the King's number. She knew his address.

Two hundred years before that, you may remember the story of Helen of Troy, known as "the face that launched a thousand ships." She was the most beautiful woman in Sparta, which is in ancient Greece. Menelaus, the king, was her husband. While he was away on a trip to a funeral, she fell in love with a drop-dead hunk named Paris and ran away with him across the Aegean Sea to Troy. Sparta launched a ten-year war to get her back! Including the famous Trojan horse trick to break into and conquer the city of Troy. In the siege, Paris died. Helen's beauty didn't save her. She was returned to Sparta to face a death sentence.

Please understand, I'm not saying beauty is altogether Shinola. Outward beauty is natural, God-given, though there's always been a thriving market of artificial enhancements. But compared to an inner, lasting beauty, outward appearances don't even take the bronze medal. Of course, the world places gold medal standards on physical beauty. But the Lord has a different approach.

> Man looks on the outward appearance,
> but the Lord looks at the heart.
>
> 1 Samuel 16:7

Apparently, singer-songwriter John Maher agrees. He put good looks in perspective this way.

> If you're pretty, you're pretty; but the only way to be beautiful is to be loving. Otherwise, it's just "congratulations about your face."

In other words, virtue is the inner beauty of a drop-dead heart. Add to that integrity, authenticity, a moral compass, and that's a real prize. Outer beauty is a genetic lottery. Virtue is a choice.

The good news is anyone can become beautiful on the inside. Even those who have blown it badly. Any of us. Like King David. Even after his adultery and arranging to have Bathsheba's husband killed in battle, God still called him a "man after his own heart." Why? How is that possible? Because he repented when he did wrong and loved God with all his heart. He reset his soul on true north. (See the letter: Character vs. Charisma.)

Here's a more recent story. We love the movie Beauty and the Beast. Belle is a beauty inside and out. Gaston is a hunk with a beastly heart. The Beast, because of a curse, looks beastly but has a drop-dead, though hidden and wounded heart. At first, the

Beast's appearance horrifies Belle. But she is slowly drawn to his loving heart and ways. He even risks and nearly loses his life for her. You know the rest. Her love for him breaks the curse. Gaston, a hunk with a beastly heart gets what he deserves. Belle gets a hunk with a drop-dead heart. It's a win-win.

My all-around, drop-dead beauties, physical attraction is wonderful, fantastic, one of the joys of this life. But I continue to hope and pray you learn sooner than later to see more than skin deep, beyond and below desires and outward features - that you each find a drop-dead gorgeous heart to love and live out your days with - someone who has an inner light from a higher, non-romantic fire, and also turns you on. (See the letter: True Love vs. Infatuation) I pray you each find someone loving, tender, true, and kind, who can say "I'm sorry." And even better, "Please forgive me." (See the letter: Forgiveness vs. Apology)

Willow, I never wrote that drop-dead heart song, so here's a stab at a chorus:

I'm lookin' for a drop-dead heart
Shallow, photogenic posers need not apply
So, don't leave a number, don't even try
Cause you don't have a shot in the dark
I'm lookin for a drop-dead heart
What good is a face that can launch an armada
If the heart and soul behind it are - full of nada?
Hey, it may sound crazy, but wherever you are
I'm lookin' for a drop-dead heart

Hey, is this crazy? Only give your number and heart to someone who has a heart after God's own. To match yours. I look forward to meeting them.

Love, Dad

Letter 9

Kind vs. *Nice*

Saruman believes it is only great power that can hold evil in check,
but that is not what I have found. I found it is the small everyday
deeds of ordinary folk that keep the darkness at bay - small acts
of kindness and love.

Gandalf, from The Hobbit by J.R.R. Tolkien

My kind kids,

There's a surefire way to recognize the difference between kind
and nice: acts of kindness are remembered a lot longer.

Sawyer, remember the Christmas you wanted a trampoline? But
Santa couldn't swing it? Some dear friends heard you wanted one
and made it happen. Christmas morning, a trampoline appeared
in our backyard. You learned to do backflips from that kindness.

Wyatt, remember our trip to California when you were ten? A
friend in Colorado connected with a racing team gave us tickets
and pit passes to the Firestone Grand Prix?

Willow, I still sleep under the beautiful blanket you crocheted
me. You spent many hours and your own money to make it.

Kindness, like joy, goes on long after the act of kindness is done.

One thing I often said to you as I dropped you off at school is,
"Be kind and be awesome. You can't be awesome if you can't be
kind."

Ever wonder why I never said, "Be nice?"

There's a big difference. Being nice is a mannerism, like social grease, to make things between people run smoother. It's mostly an outward display, usually verbal. Being nice is pleasant, but if not sincere, it's Shinola. Granted, niceness can make the world a better place. Simply saying "hello" is a nice thing to do. But any salesperson can act pleasant or courteous. So can any politician, child-nabber or even a serial killer.

Kindness and niceness can overlap, of course. Opening a door for someone carrying an armful of packages or struggling on crutches is both kind and nice. The kind part is the action driven by compassion and care for someone. Unlike mere niceness, kindness requires not only seeing a need or desire, but meeting it. Being nice usually costs very little. Kindness often requires time, effort and sometimes great sacrifice.

My grandmother Myrtle, born in 1985, told me something her childhood sweetheart and first husband, Will, did. It was late summer 1926 in Oklahoma. A little boy down the street from them came down with typhus. He was burning up with fever. His bedroom was on the sunny side of the house. This was before air conditioning. Will spent one morning building an awning over the boy's window to keep his room from getting so hot. She tried to convince Will not to go down there. But he went. The boy survived. A few weeks later, Will came down with typhus. The doctor thought he probably got it from drinking out of a stream while hunting. Myrtle insisted he got it from visiting that boy. A few weeks later, October 26, 1926, Will died in Myrtle's arms.

* * *

I have been on the receiving end of many kindnesses. The kindness I have given has brought me more than I gave, not in reciprocity, but in blessing and satisfaction. Kindness gives to the recipient and the giver.

In the big picture, as Gandalf described, there is great power in kindness. Even the most hardened heart can soften and crack under its influence. And it crosses all kinds of barriers, where other means fail.

> Kindness is a language the deaf can hear and
> the blind can see.
>
> Mark Twain

Like gratitude and humility, kindness is a mark of a transformed heart. Remember Ebenezer Scrooge? Once his icy heart thawed, kindness was his first impulse. He sent a boy to buy the biggest turkey in the market for the Cratchit family Christmas dinner.

Being kind also combats a habitual tendency in all of us – too much focus on ourselves. It moves our attention outside of us. Niceness comes from an external expectation of common courtesy, like window dressing. Kindness rises from within. It builds character and comes from character. These are two reasons your mother and I urge you to be kind. Otherness and character. (See the letters: Usie vs. Selfie, and Character vs. Charisma)

Every day, someone who crosses your path will need a little

kindness. And they will not forget it. And you will not soon forget the kindness shown to you.

One act of kindness can go a long, long way.

After my freshman year of college, at the end of a summer job as a youth intern at a church, the congregation surprised me with a money tree. That September, I was scheduled to have surgery on my back for scoliosis. I would miss an entire year of college. My first good guitar, a Gibson J-45 sunburst, had been stolen from my car outside a music store in Amarillo. With the money those kind people gave me, I bought a Martin D-35, a classic, keep-for-life instrument. That was before I ever thought about moving to Nashville and making a life in music. While recuperating, I played that guitar every day. A friend invited me the next year to join a band at a different college. That guitar traveled all over the place with us. The gift from those thoughtful people multiplied. I still have it. I've written over two thousand songs on it and carried it all over the world. I made a living with it for a very long time. And I hope a difference.

Kindness can be small or extravagant. Inviting someone at school to sit with you at lunch. Mowing someone's yard while they are on vacation. Committing a few dollars a month to an organization that helps our veterans or supports a child somewhere in the world.

Some kindnesses are very close to home.

Just after my 50th birthday, a good friend, musician, great songwriter and artist, Bruce Carroll, came over to visit. I met him in the driveway. He had a guitar case in his hand.

I said, "Oh, good. You brought your guitar."

He said, "No. I brought yours."

Very few serious guitarists in Nashville ever utter the sentence, "I don't need another guitar," but I really didn't need another one. Friends had just pitched in on my birthday to give me a fantastic Lowden acoustic guitar made in Ireland.

But Bruce "Above and Beyond" Carroll wanted me to have his McPherson, a magnificent instrument totally beyond my budget! The guitar maker, Matt Macpherson, was making it possible for Bruce to get another one, so Bruce wanted me to have his. He joked that any songs I got out of that guitar, he owned a portion of the copyright. We've written many songs together, so in a way, he got his bargain.

One last story and I'm done.

* * *

Leading up to Christmas a couple of years after that, I got sick with a chronic case of bronchitis. For more than two months, I coughed and lost sleep. Sawyer, you weren't even on the planet yet. Times were challenging. Returning from an errand I stopped at our mailbox. Among the junk mail and bills was a large manilla envelope and a letter from our church. Your mother met me inside. She was very excited. She told me my brother Brad had overnighted $2500 as a gift! Mind blown! I opened the letter from the church. There was a $500 check! Mind blown again. Our Paster said at Christmas people give anonymously to meet needs he might be aware of. He passed their kindness along to us.

People can be so kind.

But the shower of kindness didn't stop there. We gathered around the kitchen table, including your mother's mom and dad and her two young cousins who were visiting. The outside of the large manilla envelope had no postmark. Only a hand-drawn stamp in colored pencil. Obviously, it had not been mailed. Someone secretly snuck it into our mailbox. A note on the outside read, "A friend sticks closer than a brother." I opened it and dumped the contents on the table – a landslide of hundred-dollar bills tumbled out! Willow and Wyatt, you started counting. One thousand. Two thousand. Five. Eight! $10,000! Remember our amazement? Within about thirty minutes, thirteen thousand dollars was on our kitchen table! I had no idea how all these kind people knew our situation. And no idea who they were, except for my brother.

As some TV offers say, "But wait. There's more!" Your Papa Frank pulled out yet another envelope. A few weeks earlier, he requested an unspoken prayer in his men's Sunday School in Florida. One man asked him if it concerned a need they might meet. Frank told them about our rough patch. The men took up a collection on the spot. $343. We were in awe, like the five thousand people Jesus fed from five loaves and two fish! A lot of bread was on our kitchen table.

To top it all off. As all this was happening, the TV was on in the living room. The movie *It's a Wonderful Life* was playing! You can't make this stuff up or make it happen. I truly felt like George Bailey, "the richest man in town." A lot of angels got their wings that day. And our hearts were flying.

I still have that manilla envelope. And the story and the joy of those great kindnesses.

* * *

So, my earth angels, whether it's holding a door for someone, paying for the person behind you at a drive-through window, or an anonymous gift, big or small, it's no wonder kindness made the top nine. What's the top nine? The nine fruits of the Spirit listed in Galatians 5:22.

But the fruit of the Spirit is love, joy, peace, forbearance, kindness, goodness, faithfulness, gentleness and self-control.

As you can see, niceness, though generally a good thing, did not make the list.

Love, Dad

Letter 10

Christmas vs. *Holiday*

Til He appeared, and the soul felt its worth.

from O Holy Night

Bah, humbug!

Ebenezer Scrooge

My year-round elves,

There are two kinds of people in the world. The lost. And the "I once was lost but now I'm found." Christmas is for both. For the found, it's a celebration. For the lost, it's just another holiday, a pagan ritual shoplifted by Christians from ancient ceremonies around the winter solstice, the shortest day of the year, to mark the annual beginning of longer daylight. For the found, Christmas celebrates the light of the world, the Christ child, miraculously coming into his own creation, bringing, or at least offering, peace on earth and affirming God's good will toward all of us.

Every Christmas morning since you were very little, we've read the story from Luke chapter 2 about the birth of Jesus. We still do that. We always will. I hope you and your children read it, too.

When you think about it, it's odd that we give presents to each other even though Christmas is not our birthday. But we are not the first culture to make a buck off the Lord. Even with all the commerce surrounding Christmas, at its core is Christ.

But not for a lot of people. As you've grown up, the Humbugs and their lawyers have grown louder and shrewder. Christmas trees and Nativity scenes have been banned from schools and public places. While you were losing your baby teeth, learning to read and write and ride your bikes, the government of the people, by the people and for the people increasingly became a government of the humbugs, by the humbugs and for the humbugs. They haven't let up. And are not likely to.

Even saying, "Merry Christmas" is offensive to humbugs. If you ever work at a place where the owners or managers forbid you to say "Merry Christmas" to customers or staff, you could get your own good lawyer and maybe make a better living suing them for restricting your first amendment rights, or just wish them "Merry Christmas," and work somewhere else.

Here's a hard reality. It may be difficult for you to believe, but some people prefer darkness and shadow to light. Tuck that away. Observe people. You are elf-aware enough to spot this. (I couldn't resist that.) I won't list the kinds of darkness going on all around us in the name of personal freedom and elf-expression (I did it again. Not sorry.) You can see it for yourself.

> "The light has come into the world,
> but people loved darkness more than the light."

> John 3:19

Hard to imagine, isn't it? Preferring darkness to light. But very smart, well-educated humbugs especially, prefer being enlightened to walking in the light. (See the letter: Wisdom vs. Education.)

But not to worry my eagle-eyed elves, Christmas is not about outward displays or who has the more clever lawyer.

A line in the Christmas song, "Joy to the World," gets to the heart of the matter.

> Let every heart prepare him room.
>
> from *Joy to the World*

God wants every heart to make room for him, not just decorate a room with a tree, or string lights on our houses and main street, or place a Nativity scene in a park or on the lawn of the White House. Even if we could do all that, those are only outward signs of an inner reality. We can put bumper stickers on our cars urging others to "Keep Christ in Christmas." That's a fine reminder. But even without bumper stickers, we can make room for him. And as long as we make room in our hearts for Christ, the humbugs cannot legislate, agitate or excavate Christmas from us individually, or from a nation where many millions carry Christmas in their hearts. And in many more hearts all around the world. Might as well ask a bird not to sing, long for the sky, don't use your wings, right? NOT gonna happen.

The world doesn't need another holiday. The world needs Christmas. Because the world needs Christ. The light has come. In spite of a determined campaign against that light and the true reason for the season, some humbug hearts make room for him. That's our prayer. And the mission and hope of the babe in Bethlehem.

* * *

Let me tell a humbug story. Willow and Wyatt, when you were very young, before Sawyer was born, we had two neighbors, a couple, who were humbugs. Not rude or combative, just unbelievers. Lost, but very pleasant, good neighbors. Both extremely bright. Both scientists. The wife, let's call her Sally, did research in antivenom treatments for poisonous snakebites. Her husband, let's call him Earl, did research in microbiology. Earl believed humans are just the sum of all our parts, no more, no less, and someday, science would unlock all our parts and be able to fix anything that broke down. Any disease. Any damaging condition.

It came to pass that Sally and Earl welcomed their first child, a little girl. When she wrapped her little hand around Earl's finger, he explained it very objectively, as merely an auto-electro-chemical response in her. Get the picture? A scientist to the core.

One day, Sally had to fly away for a few days to defend her research protocol to the FDA (Food and Drug Administration). It was her first time away from her little girl. When Sally returned, she was different. She told us why.

Several months earlier, someone had given her a book about the historical evidence surrounding Jesus. She was a researcher. So, she read it. On her business trip, one evening in her hotel room, she "chanced" upon a Christian program raising support for hungry children around the world. Because she now had a little girl, the need moved her. She called the number on the screen to make a donation. After she did, the kind voice on the other end of the line asked if she had a prayer request. Sally, to her own surprise, said, "I think I want to become a Christian. How do I do that?" She got down on her knees in that hotel room. The person prayed with her. The scientist and new mother made room in her heart and put her faith and life in the hands of Jesus.

Sally told us from that moment she saw everything different - creation, science, her identity, her place in the universe. We marveled and laughed with her. We had been praying for Sally and Earl.

Then she said, "Pray for Earl. He's going to be a hard nut to crack."

A few weeks later, on a Sunday afternoon, we invited Sally and Earl over for lunch. We weren't going to bring up the happy elephant in the room. But as they say, out of the mouth of babes, Willow, you blurted out, "Mr. Earl, Ms. Sally turned into a Christian."

Awkward silence.

As Earl fed their baby next to him, he broke the tension with a droll, "I know, Willow. I know."

I couldn't hold back a laugh. We all laughed. Except Earl. I still chuckle thinking about it.

Sally found a church. Sunday mornings Earl watched their daughter at home while Sally attended. She even joined the worship team.

Not long after, we moved. They moved. We lost touch. I don't know if Earl has made room in his heart. I pray he has, or will.

Sally's awakening didn't happen at Christmas. But the light of Christmas has no solstice. It shines steady, all year long.

* * *

Clearly, my dears, no army of humbug lawyers can ever outlaw Christmas in our hearts. No cultural bullying can censor "Merry Christmas" from our lips. But how do humbugs become believers? Not from how we prevail in debates or court. (Though some battles can be fought and won in just courts.) Not merely from "Merry Christmas" on our lips, or sweet gifts on Christmas morning. And probably not so much from the chrome fish and stickers on our bumpers, like the edgy one I saw that read: "Happy Winter Solstice. Have a nice day in the futile darkness of paganism." God save us from the ministry of sarcasm.

It's clear the lost can become found. It's been happening for over two-thousand years - to religious hard heads like the Apostle Paul, struck blind on the road to Damascus, to hard-hearted humbugs like John Newton, the cruel English captain of a slave ship. During a violent storm at sea, his thoughts turned to his mother's faith. He repented of his wicked ways. His stony heart cracked and made room for the Lord. He even became a minister and wrote one of the most famous songs in the world.

> Amazing grace, how sweet the sound
> That saved a wretch like me,
> I once was lost, but now I'm found,
> Was blind but now I see.

They say God moves in mysterious ways. It doesn't take being struck blind or a life-threatening storm. Some of his ways are not

64

mysterious at all. The Lord made them plain. We are reminded, "God's kindness leads us to repentance." Roman 2:4. (See the letter: Kind vs. Nice) He put two other winning ways clearly in our hands: "Love one another." And "Love your neighbor as yourself."

Even humbugs have no compelling argument against kindness, love and compassion.

Sawyer, from a very young age, you had a sincere and direct way with strangers. You still do with some of your buddies. In a music story one day, I was paying for some guitar strings. Within the clerk's hearing, you asked me if the very tall, edgy-looking, rock and roll man behind the counter was a Christian. I said, "Why don't you ask him?" You looked up with those baby blues and asked him sweetly, "Are you a Christian?" The man beamed down at you, said yes, that he loved Jesus with all his heart. You smiled and said, "That's good." Even if he had not been, I'm sure your tender approach would have gently planted a seed in the soil of his soul.

I remember when God cracked open my heart. Church camp. June after my sophomore year in high school. Thursday night was silent night until breakfast the next morning. No one could say a word. That's a very tall order for teenagers, but we didn't have mobile phones to cheat with. The assignment: listen for the voice of the God. I didn't know how that worked and was pretty sure I would come up empty. I sat for a long time on a picnic table out under billions of stars, feeling smaller than a molecule and invisible. From out of nowhere, three words came into my mind. "You are mine." They repeated, "You are mine." I knew it was the Lord. He found me out there in the big empty of West Texas and my heart made room for him.

I also remember the days each of you made room in your hearts for the Christ of Christmas. Those dates are written down. I remember baptizing each of you. He's cracked open all our hearts with his kindness, mercy and grace. That is joy to my world.

* * *

When it comes to Christmas and Christ, we need to remember, there's no 'us' and 'them.' The tidings of great joy are for all the world. Jesus said he came to seek and save the lost. That's all of us. But each one of us decides to stay lost or be found.

> The people walking in darkness have seen a great light;
> on those living in darkness a light has dawned.
>
> Isaiah 9:2

It's encouraging to know, if stony humbugs like the Apostle Paul, John Newton, and Ebenezer Scrooge can go from lost to found, from darkness to light, the Lord can crack any nut.

My beautiful nutcrackers, as we walk in the light, let's lead with kindness, love and compassion. That's how the Lord pursued us. He didn't come to give us a holiday. Who needs a holiday… when we can have the joy and hope of Christmas? Right? Like I said, bumper stickers won't change the world much, but I'd still like to see one that reads:

Love one another. Hug a Humbug!

Love, Dad

Letter 11

Savior vs. *Hero*

We don't need another hero.

Tina Turner

My three superheroes,

From the very start, we all need heroes. To hold our hand crossing the street. Bandage a scraped knee. Teach us to tie our shoes. How to read. Hold us when our heart hurts. Nurse us in sickness. Cheer us on when we win or lose. The whole world needs heroes. To face bullies on the playground and defeat tyrants and criminals in our neighborhoods, our nation and around the world. And especially, to show us what courage is. (See Letter 4: Courage vs. Bravado)

I have some heroes in my life. Besides you.

Virginia Saucier, my Sunday school teacher. Ron Lowe, our youth director. Mrs. Thompson, my eighth-grade science teacher. Dr. Tom Copeland, a professor at TCU whose passion for literature fed my own. Michael Blanton, a college friend whose vision opened the door to my life calling. This is a short list of my heroes. There are many more.

None of them could leap tall buildings at a single bound, run faster than a speeding bullet, had X-ray vision, or could fly without an airplane. None of them rescued me from a burning building or a sinking car. But they all had superpowers: love, caring, kindness, encouragement and wisdom. Each of them shaped me and changed the quality and course of my life.

You will have your own list of heroes. Friends, teachers, leaders, mentors. (Maybe a songwriter with a moustache?)

You have your own list of superheroes, too. Superman, Batman, Spiderman, The Incredibles, the Avengers and more. How many times did we watch those movies?

The whole superhero thing goes back a long way. For thousands of years, people have imagined death-defying, immortal protectors with superhuman powers able to come to the rescue against impossible odds. The Greeks created the myth of Hercules, an early avenger of sorts. They imagined an array of fictional, powerful beings, like Poseidon, ruler of the sea. Artemis, with her deadly bow and arrows, could turn herself and others into animals. She had the power of healing, too. Hermes, called Mercury by the Romans, had wings on his feet to deliver messages with great speed from the gods in heaven to mortals on earth and in the realm of the dead. He would have made a spectacular soccer player. We just dress him different and call him "the Flash."

Some heroes are mere mortals. David slew Goliath. The founders of America stood against the goliath of Britain. Nelson Mandela led the defeat of apartheid in South Africa. All of them had feet of clay, flaws. But rose to the challenge of their times.

All the human heroes I'm aware of were prepared for that role through heartache, sacrifice and suffering. I'm sorry to have to tell you, you will go through those fires on your way to becoming a hero for someone else. That just seems to be the way it works. One of the great mysteries is how God's power pours through weakness and adversity. Though you may not see it now, I am confident your names will be added to someone's list of heroes.

But, my future legends, there are some adversaries no hero can defeat and save us from. Only one death-defying immortal protector can rescue our souls. I believe you know where this is headed.

A hero can lead us or a nation through upheaval and conflict.

Only a Savior can lead us in the way everlasting.

A hero can save the day.

It takes a Savior to save our souls.

A hero can rescue us from physical danger.

Only a Savior can rescue us from ourselves, our sin, guilt, shame, and hell.

A hero can bring healing skill to a broken bone or aching back.

But only a Savior can heal the brokenness and ache in our spirit, when our heart is shattered by rejection, betrayal, or buried under an avalanche of grief.

Before I met your mother, you know I loved a beautiful and bright woman, Rosalynn. We were planning to be married. Five months before that, on a Saturday morning the week before Thanksgiving, she died instantly in a car wreck on her way to see me. Devastating. World-shattering. The following Monday I got a letter from her, sent the day before she died. She signed it, "Press on." Easy said. Beyond difficult to do.

So many personal heroes walked with me through that dark season. They were a great strength and comfort. Someone cleaned and restocked my refrigerator. I still have no idea who did such a kind thing. I entered a long valley, and got stuck, convinced the pain would never go away. I thought the wrestling match with the God I followed and trusted would not be resolved in this life. I understood how people with a deep wound just trudge and endure, white knuckling their case against God. Another good and rich season ahead was hard to imagine.

Many heroes, familiar with deep sorrow, walked with me. But no hero could have delivered me from the valley of the deep shadow of death. Only a Savior who walked that valley himself could do that. And he did. I describe how he did that in "Letter to a Grieving Heart," a book written to help others walking that valley. Because of a Savior, not a hero, another good and rich season came, including love and marriage and the matchless blessings of you, my flesh and blood treasures.

I have to tell you straight up - other heartaches and challenging days are ahead that will require more than a hero. Jesus wasn't just theorizing when he said, "In this world you will have trouble." Thankfully, he didn't stop there. He said something no mortal hero can say, "But take heart, for I have overcome the world." This includes him defeating nemesis number one: death. Even a fictional hero like Ironman couldn't pull that off. Death is the kryptonite of every human hero. But not for our Savior.

It comes down to this. If we don't have a soul, if there is not a God who saves, there's no need for a Savior. In that case, the entire world would have to settle for heroes to rescue us from troubles, and avert the catastrophes of the day. Even more dire, without a Savior who would hold the hopelessness, emptiness and heartache at bay? Eloquent poets and songwriters? (See the letter: Heaven vs. Sky) The next exciting lover? Doctors and scientists can't come up with a hope pill. Self-help gurus and late-night funny guys only help us whistle and chuckle in the dark. And obviously, we can't put our hope in the worst counterfeit heroes of our time, politicians. (See the letter: Leader vs Politician)

Sometimes we all need someone to save the day, a human hero. Thank God for them. I am grateful to have human heroes in my corner.

As for superheroes, besides entertainment, their only benefit I see is this: they point to the longing in our soul for a real, immortal, invincible champion, able to deliver us even from death, and make the object of our hopes and longings a reality. Only a Savior fits that job description in real life. I don't need a superhero. I have a Savior. So grateful you do, too.

My earth angels, in the long run, facing the day to day, the come what may, and our own human nature, we all still need a Savior. All the time.

Somebody cue the song.

Love, Dad

I Still Need a Savior

My home in heaven is secure
My name is in the book of life
Even so my heart can harbor shadows
Of doubt, sin and pride

Your truth, Oh Lord, has set me free
Your love revives me like a spring
Even so I fall and have to follow
On my knees

CHORUS
I still need a Savior - Wash my hands and feet
Breathe a willing spirit - For my flesh is weak
Heal my broken places - With Your perfect peace
Watch over me, Watch over me
I Still Need a Savior - O, Lord be my strength
From Your well of wisdom - Give me words to speak
In the heat of battle - You have promised me
You'll never leave, You'll never leave... You never leave

My hope has bled on solid ground
Your grace removed my heart of stone
Even so my feet of clay will stumble
On my own

CHORUS

by me from the album, "Soundtrack of My Soul"

Letter 12

Usie vs. *Selfie*

But enough about me. Let's talk about you…what do you think of me?

CC Bloom (played by Bette Midler
in the movie "Beaches")

My winged wonders,

Remember some of our morning wake-up routines? I loved squeezing the sleepy out of your little legs and arms, out your toes and fingers. From your ears and face. Or tickling you, accusing you of hiding candy under your arms or in your rib cage? Hearing you giggle and protest was music to my ears. Sawyer, we used a saying for each weekday morning:

"His mercies are new every Monday."
"It's Twos-day, not Ones-day. Look-out-for-someone-else day."
"It's Wins-day, not Wednesday. Unless you snooze it away."
"It's Thors-day. Strong day. I can do all things through Christ who gives me strength day."
"It's Fly-day, not Friday. Some glad morning when school days are over, I'll fly away."

Our Tuesday morning slogan, Twos-day, not Ones-day, was based on the scripture:

> Do not merely look out for your own personal interests,
> but also for the interests of others.   Philippians 2:4

One of the things your mother and I tried to instill in you was "otherness." To be aware of those around you. Introduce yourself. Learn someone's name. Remember their name. Shake hands firmly and look people in the eye. Ask about them. Not just gab about yourself, what you were into or wanted to do, or some song or TV show you liked. Or "whatever." Being aware of other people requires taking the focus off ourselves. Not easy. For any of us.

You're growing up in a time when taking selfies on a phone has become a social media virus. "Here's my new haircut, or color, or ear piercing. Here's me at the mall. Here's my new clothes. Here's my moody, rock and roll 'I don't give a crap face'. Look at me crushing it on the dancefloor." Standby for more of me!

To cut you some slack, being self-obsessed didn't start with your generation. Or with mine. One anthem of my parents' generation was the hit song, "I Did It My Way." It's filled with unwavering, single-minded drive. Frank Sinatra perhaps sold it better than anyone. He made doing life "my way" sound more than admirable. Apparently, it was the north star of being human and the single highest quality of heroic character. (See the letter: Character vs. Charisma)

Advertisers use the focus on ourselves as a primary motive all the time. "Have it your way." "You deserve a break today." "Obey your thirst." "Freedom is being yourself, no matter what anyone else thinks."

Long before you came along, songwriters and recording artists repeatedly tried to tattoo self-supremacy on our psyche. Hits like:

74

It's Your Thing, Do What You Want to Do, The Isley Brothers 1969; *What Have You Done for Me Lately?* Janet Jackson 1981. In 1985, a group called "The Outfield" had a big hit song. In it, the singer's girlfriend is out of town, so he wants her friend to stay the night and keep it a secret. He's shamelessly honest about it. "I just want to use your love tonight." The song is clearly selling the Shinola of lust. The song title? Your Love. Love? Right. Anybody buying that? And of course, there's the classic, brazen, do-it-your-way smash hit: *You Gotta Fight for Your Right to Party,* Beastie Boys 1986.

But self-preoccupation goes back much farther than Sinatra.

In 1782, a year before the Revolutionary War ended, a Frenchman, Jean de Crèvecoeur, came over to observe our fledgling country and culture. In an essay called "What is an American?" he boiled the new experiment down to one basic element. America's genius, success and prosperity "is founded on the basis of nature, self-interest." In America an individual could go, do and become anything they set their mind and strength to. Six years earlier, Jefferson put self-interest front and center in the Declaration of Independence in our God-given rights to "life, liberty and the pursuit of happiness." (See the letter: Joy vs. Happiness)

I've already written to you about "Love your neighbor as yourself." (again, in the letter: Joy vs. Happiness) A balanced self-love or self-interest is born into us. Self-care. Self-preservation. Self-defense. But a life lived as if the world revolves around us would create a planet of Scrooges and Prince Charmings (or Princesses). None of us is immune from a strong imbalance toward self-preoccupation.

In my early days as a recording artist, I got a good but uncomfortable lesson in this. In pursuing a music career, there's a lot of focus on you as the artist. Interviews, promotions, marketing, conversations all focus on you: Where are you from? How did you get here? What made you write that song? Where did you get the cool shoes on your album cover? And on and on. That kind of attention can feed the ego and starve the soul. (See the letter: Dignity vs. Ego) Well, over coffee one day, a good friend gently confronted me. She pointed out that whenever we got together I didn't ask much about what her life was like and what she was going through. With the care of a true friend, she said our conversations were almost entirely about me. Talk about a wake-up call! She was right. It was a moment I badly needed. And heeded. Everyone should have a friend like that.

In a culture so fixated on self, learning it's not all about us is a hard lesson. But taking the road less traveled, toward others, out of the cul-de-sac of self, leads to a better, richer life.

> To journey for the sake of saving our own lives is little by little to cease to live… because it is only by journeying for the world's sake – even when the world bores and sickens and scares you half to death – that little by little we start to come alive.
>
> Frederick Buechner
> from "The Sacred Journey"

Look around. There's a pandemic of self-centeredness. In fact, our natural, healthy self-interest has metastasized (multiplied and spread) into terminal selfishness. It must be very crowded on the throne at the center of the universe. No wonder "I Did It My Way" is a cultural anthem.

Thank God, in so many places the contrast is clear between the selfish and the selfless. From individuals to organizations. There really are people who have busy lives but take the time to care about others. Movies made about the selfless among us draw big audiences and their stories hang around longer. *The Hiding Place. The Help. The Blindside. Driving Miss Daisy, Schindler's List,* and one of our favorites, *It's a Wonderful Life.* We know the story by heart. George Bailey lays down his dream of traveling the world to battle the richest, meanest, most selfish man in town in order to care for his family and neighbors in Bedford Falls. George's otherness actually made him the "richest man in town."

Which brings me to you. There's an old Quaker saying:

A society grows great when old men plant trees
the shade of which they know they will never sit in.

Imagine a society where young people plant the seeds of care and kindness (See the letter: Kind vs. Nice) and look out for others. A society that takes more Usies than Selfies.

I can imagine that. Because I see otherness in you and growing stronger. You know you are not the center of the universe. You don't want to settle for the hollowness of "merely" looking out for your own interests. You know life is a group hike. I'm so glad to be in your group photo. Everyone smile and say like Wyatt did early on, "Kwackers 'n Cheese."

Love, Dad

Letter 13

Joy vs. *Happiness*

> Joy is the infallible sign of the presence of God.
> Madeleine L'Engle

> … endowed by their Creator with certain inalienable Rights,
> that among these are
> Life, Liberty and the pursuit of Happiness.
> Declaration of Independence

My delights,

Joy and happiness are both good things. But not the same thing at all. Two images come to mind when I think of the difference.

First and more recent, your Aunt Karen makes a sweetbread that I've watched you devour like puppies discovering bacon. Her yummy treat is more like a dessert than a bread. I've never seen you eat any cake or brownie the way you consume her sweet bread. Eating that divine, moist, cinnamon-sugary treat makes you happy, right? And when you ask her for it, watch her slice it, sometimes heat it up and serve it up with a glass of cold milk, what happens in you is obvious: happiness, pure and simple. But you may have missed something. Because you were so focused on your pursuit of happiness, did you ever see the joy on Aunt Karen's face and hear it in her voice as she serves you her sweetbread? She loves to watch you enjoy it. It happens every time, without fail. You get the happiness, but she gets the joy.

Here's another picture of the difference between joy and happiness.

In my family, we grew up fishing with my Dad. Before we were old enough to throw a hook out by ourselves without tangling the whole world in fishing line, he used to set out a few lines from the bank or a dock. We would sit and wait, especially us boys. My two sisters mostly got bored pretty quick and pursued happiness elsewhere, picking flowers or playing in the camper out of the intense summer sun.

Here's how the scene would play out. Dad watched each line intently, keeping one eye on us so we wouldn't trip or tumble into the water. Just like I've done whenever you were near a body of water as little ones. When a fish nibbled on a line, he would carefully pick up that rod, wait for the right moment, and with a quick jerk set the hook. After making sure the fish was on the line, Dad would hand the rod to one of us to fight the beast and haul it in.

On one occasion at a lake in Oklahoma, I remember Dad hooking a fish and handing the rod to my brother, Barry. The rod immediately bent into a great arc from the weight of a pretty hefty fish. This was no bluegill perch. There was a monster on the line. Barry complained under the pressure and cried out for help. I remember laughing and taunting him, like any big brother would. And I remember Dad laughing and coaching him to keep the tip of the rod up and hold on. The drama grew more and more intense, Barry wearing down and hoping not to be pulled to a watery death. Finally, what surfaced was not one monster, but two! Dad often tied two hooks on one line. This time, it paid off. Barry hauled in two big mudcats at once! We were all whooping and hollering and beaming. Barry caught the fish. We boys got the happiness - but Dad caught the joy.

* * *

Let me get back to those two illustrations in a bit.

Let's play that game we play on the way to school sometimes: "One of these things is not like the other, and why?" Some of them were more obvious than others. For instance: Pinto beans - jelly beans - lima beans. One is a candy, right? But they got trickier, more subtle. Snow – rain - fog. They're all water, but two of them fall from the sky. One rises from the ground. Fog.

How about these three things? Life – Liberty - Pursuit of Happiness. Which one is not like the others? And why? Think about that for a bit.

I've wondered if "Happiness" was the best word Thomas Jefferson could have used in that list as he was drafting the famous Declaration of Independence. Why not the *pursuit* of "fulfillment" or "purpose" or "destiny?" The God-given right he actually framed was the pursuit of happiness, not happiness itself. In earlier drafts, Jefferson wrote: "We hold these truths to be *sacred & undeniable.*"

I also wonder if the three rights he named are in order of priority. What order would you put them in? Life first and foremost? Maybe Liberty next? If you don't have life, you can't have liberty, right? If you have Life but not Liberty, and those places exist today, you can't really pursue Happiness very freely.

Have I given you enough to answer which one is not like the others? Life, right? Why? Because it's the one you have to have to make the other two possible. And Liberty is necessary to make the *pursuit* of Happiness possible.

Today, lots of people flip the order, placing a priority on each of the three rights to reflect their worldview (which is how someone sees the world). For those who believe personal freedom is the highest right, the list would read, "Liberty, Life, Happiness." For those willing to give up some liberties as long as they are happy, their order of importance might be "Happiness, Life, and Liberty." As odd and illogical as it may seem, others prefer a world where Happiness and Liberty take precedent over the right to Life itself. That's part of what the great divide about abortion rests on. Which right is most sacred? Life, Liberty or the pursuit of Happiness?

Believe it or not, you are already living in a time where some countries and states grant individuals the liberty to end their own lives, assisted by medical professionals. You heard me right. The liberty to forfeit happiness and life itself becomes the highest right for some. "Liberty, Happiness, Life." This issue has a big word, "euthanasia." It means allowing and assisting in the painless killing of a person who has decided life in a certain condition is not worth living. For now, this is illegal in most places. But that view is spreading.

These situations are certainly excruciating. They pit mercy against the sanctity of life, in any condition. A very tough issue. Being in excruciating pain might make anyone rearrange the priorities. That's what living wills are for - when someone is beyond communicating and reviving.

Let me point out, once life ceases to be sacred in one circumstance, silver-tongued Shinola peddlers can play a shell game, especially in the medical field and in the courts. And it's happening. When does life begin? When does it end? Just add a few words and it gets very slippery. When does *viable* human life begin? Does *quality* of life determine its value? Already, a few countries make it possible for mentally ill patients to choose euthanasia, instead of getting medical help. And some take the view that a prenatal baby with a range of abnormalities can be aborted. It's even being debated whether an abortion should be an option if the unborn child is not of the gender parents prefer!

This is the "modern" world you've been born into, where life, liberty and pursuit of happiness mean different things to different people.

Well, how did I get from sweet bread to euthanasia? You know me so well that probably doesn't surprise you. Those heavy issues may seem a long way from the difference between joy and happiness, but this is why words have meaning. And the meaning and priority of things shape our lives.

For instance, many people conveniently drop the phrase "pursuit of" in Jefferson's statement. There is a growing view that by simply being born, we have a right to be happy - not a right to *pursue* happiness. Can you see how the term *pursuit* of ties happiness to Liberty? You have to have a measure of freedom to pursue happiness. But the right to *pursue* doesn't guarantee happiness. Even so, some people have a worldview that the government or more productive people in society should insure their happiness and wellbeing. The clamor for that resembles a room full of two-year-olds fighting over Aunt Karen's sweetbread. I'm happy to report you three never resorted to that. Well done. (Of course, there was always plenty to go around.)

By "happiness" does anyone really think Thomas Jefferson meant selfishness or even simple self-interest above all other values, even above the right to life? The view "I'm here so I deserve happiness" places an individual in the center of the universe - that it really is all about you. You don't have to look far to see it. In one of her first big hits, the singer Janet Jackson sang "What have you done for me lately?" Another fabulously wealthy star of film and television told an interviewer, "I've reached a place in my life where I only do what I want to do when I want to do it." Sounds desirable, doesn't it? And she has a right to pursue that. But is that admirable? And will it keep her happy? (See more about this in the letters: Significance vs. Success and Usie vs. Selfie)

Here's another sign of a growing self-centered worldview that sells happiness, but is less likely to reap joy.

When I was a kid, my favorite magazine was called *Life*. It had fantastic pictures of places and people and animals and events from around the whole world, from the rich variety of life and cultures on this planet. I remember reading every page with great curiosity and wonder. Over the decades, magazines became more specific. *Life* magazine gave way to *People*. Then Us came along. More recently, magazines like *Self* and *Moi* (French for "Me") appeared on the scene. Meanwhile, in the internet world, MySpace, Facebook, Twitter, Instagram and others have created a personal, moment by moment "magazine" focused almost entirely on me, myself and I. Now the entire planet can have a window into the most important, fascinating, bigger than life, center of the universe, person - me. The planet can know what I eat, read, think, wear - what brings me happiness.

* * *

Let's be clear, my dears, love of self is not totally a negative. It depends on the degree of self-love. In the extreme, love of self above all others is called narcissism, after the Greek god Narcissus. He loved the way he looked so much that he stared at his reflection in a pool, lost his balance, fell in and drowned! He lost it all: happiness, liberty, and life. You'd think that would be a warning to movie and music stars and public figures who obsess on their own images on electronic screens all over the world. They say love is blind. Apparently, narcissism is blind and potentially deadly. Narcissism goes beyond self-love to self-worship.

Jesus made it clear that love of self is natural, a given. He said, "Love your neighbor as yourself." That assumes we look out pretty well for our own well-being. But he called us to apply that kind of care to our neighbor, too. That's known around the world as the golden rule. "Do unto others as you would have them do for you." (in Matthew 7) But Jesus also clearly balanced this, saying, "Deny your*self*," and "Whoever finds his life will lose it, and whoever loses his life for my sake will find it."

So, what does all this have to do with joy and happiness?

Well, take "Aunt" Karen's sweet bread. What if she made it,

never gave it away and ate it all herself? It might make her very happy - and very large. But that's not why she makes it. In fact, have you ever seen her eat much of it? She makes it for the delight of others.

And what about my dad's hook-and-pass-the-rod kind of fishing? I know he loved catching fish himself. What if he had just let us watch him pull in those monster catfish and bass? It might have made him happy - but he landed a much bigger catch – joy.

What I'm getting at is not an instruction against being happy, but a caution about making happiness your driving force. If the pursuit of happiness is at the center of your day, your activities, your emotions, and your worldview, you will, like too many people, settle for less.

For example, every Christmas we hear the expression, "It's more blessed or better to give than receive." But most of us, especially as children, make a long list of what we want to get for Christmas. That list is usually a lot longer than the list of what we plan to *give*. And in focusing on getting, we settle for happiness when we could have joy.

Maybe most people don't know or have forgotten that there is a much better pursuit than happiness, one with a richer payoff. Maybe people have not yet discovered that happiness is a by-product, that it actually happens when you don't focus on it as the primary goal. To look at our culture, it's easy to get the defeated feeling that we have passed the tipping point toward a self-driven, self-obsessed, extremely selfish society. That we are mainly concerned with the personal pursuit of happiness, pleasure and power and believe we are entitled to it - simply because we are alive.

I still like to believe most people, deep down, know that joy is more sacred than the pursuit of happiness. The success of many great movies reflects this. *The Blind Side. The Help, Life is Beautiful, Up, Elephant Man* (one of my favorites), *It's a Wonderful Life.* All these stories bring that reality to the surface in millions of people - the deeper reality that joy is found in giving, in sacrifice, in doing for and loving others, often at the cost of personal happiness, safety and sometimes even life. Millions of people still respond deeply to these kinds of lives and stories. Maybe there is still hope for a wakeup call.

* * *

I'm almost done. (Does that make you happy? ;) Here are some ways to tell if what you are pursuing and experiencing is happiness or joy.

 – Happiness mostly flows from outside in. "Look at my new shoes!" "I got a raise!" "I won the lottery!"
 – Joy generally flows from the inside out. "You're welcome." "I know how you like ice cream, and it was on my way." "Glad I could help."
 – Happiness is most often tied to external conditions.
 – Joy is more internal, deeper and often fueled by the happiness or well-being of someone else.

There are exceptions to this, of course. Like the joy of a job well done. The joy of accomplishing a personal goal. The joy of being truly loved by someone - by God himself.

Whatever the source, joy and happiness have certain characteristics.

Happiness is shorter than joy. Happiness is fairly local in time and space.

Joy lasts longer and resists the erosion of time and location. Just the thought of that sweet bread and Aunt Karen can bring you joy right now, even when you are not with her and there is no sweet bread within reach. I can close my eyes and still hear the echo of my dad's laugh and Barry's complaints trying to land those fish.

Happiness passes. Joy endures.

What if Thomas Jefferson had not chosen the phrase "pursuit of happiness"? What if he had chosen something like - "the right to the possibility of joy"? No doubt people would still interpret that to suit their own agenda, just as they are doing today. In any case, the difference is clear.

So, my joy-makers, when given the choice between pursuing happiness or joy - pursue the things that bring joy. And the joy in your own lives can speak volumes to a world seeking happiness in a million different ways.

The prophet Nehemiah did not write, "Happiness is your strength." He wrote, "The joy of the Lord is your strength." My hope is this. That you aim your lives, earlier than I did, at a storyline marked by the pursuit of joy instead of your own happiness. I predict you will find that happiness will come - and go - but the joy will still be sweet long after the fried catfish and sweet bread are gobbled down.

Love, Dad

Letter 14

Wisdom vs. *Education*

A learned fool is sillier than an ignorant one.   Moliere

The one who gets wisdom loves life. Solomon - Proverbs 19:8

My luminous legacy,

In my university years, especially the two spent in graduate school, a key unspoken motto (prevailing clandestine proverb) in the Literature department was: "If there exists a more grandiose descriptor, by all means employ it." Translation: If there's a bigger word, use it.

My common-sense children, beware of those who say "prevaricate" instead of "lie"; "obfuscate" rather than "blur." A favorite word switch of Shinola purveyors (sellers) is "invest" when they really mean "spend", and usually your money, not theirs. (See the letter: Leader vs. Politician)

Don't use words too big for the subject. Don't say 'infinitely' when you mean 'very',otherwise, you'll have no word left when you want to talk about something really infinite.

-C.S. Lewis

Don't get me wrong. You know I love and enjoy words. They can bring heart, vitality, power, playfulness, clarity, and precision.

88

Example: Here's something we say to each other a lot. "You're the best." That can be spiced up (amplified) with wordplay. "You are the most splendificatious." Or it can be said poetically. "In my eyes you just might be the highest mountain or the tallest tree."

Wordplay and poetry are not necessarily attempts to sell something false or less than. A key method of poetry is approaching things indirectly. A poet attempts to unveil something in terms of another thing. "My love is like a red, red rose."(Robert Burns) Generally, poetry is not an attempt to deceive but to reveal (illuminate) something deep, powerful and worth noticing, something beyond the ability of words to capture adequately. So, a good poet word-paints with fresh combinations of words and images to spark insight (ignite sagaciousness) or an "a ha" (eureka) response in the reader.

The Shinola peddler may certainly use wordplay or poetry, but the objective is often a "gotcha" effect. Depending on how words are chosen, they can be a reliable compass or a subtle shell game.

Compare these bits of poetry and song lyrics.

Roses are red, violets are blue
Love blossoms best when colors are true.
(I made that one up myself)

There's a rose in a fisted glove and the eagle flies
with the dove.
If you can't be with the one you love, honey, love
the one you're with.

Stephen Stills - songwriter

Just remember in the winter far beneath the bitter snows
Lies the seed that with the sun's love in the spring becomes
the rose.   Amanda McBroom songwriter

Can you spot the Shinola? Each poet uses the word "love", but does it mean the same thing in each? Obviously, the Shinola is sandwiched in the middle. Stephen Stills is clearly talking about lust, not love. Pure Shinola. Often it will not be this easy to sniff out (discern).

This example also illustrates one way to recognize Shinola peddlers. They often question the definition of words and change them to suit their own purpose. This can be especially true of the highly educated. If you say "up" they might say, "it depends on what you mean by 'up'." If you say "love" they tend to have many variations of what "love" is. They replace "grace" with their synonym "tolerance." (See the letter: Grace vs. Tolerance) If you mean "steal" they might translate (metamorphose or euphemize) that to "live off the land" or "share the wealth." The old saying, "If you mean what you say, say what you mean" is completely lost on a Shinolator, who twists the meanings words to gain some advantage.

Likewise, the skillful Shinola peddler does not prefer or practice directness. You will notice this in many highly educated people and especially in politicians. They almost never answer a direct question with a direct answer. (More on this in the letter: Leader vs. Politician) Instead of clearing the air, the Shinola peddler creates a smoke screen with language often to blur (obfuscate) true motives, the truth itself or both.

For instance, let's say the question is asked: "Are you in favor of the proposal?" A direct response could be either, "Yes, completely in favor," or "No, I do not support the proposal." Another direct and honest response might be, "I am still undecided and want more information." A far less than direct response polished in Shinola might be, "I am not unsympathetic to entertaining or reviewing the proposal." Likely translation: "I am not in favor of the current proposal as written but don't want to appear uncooperative or at odds with anyone and actually want to defeat the proposal by delaying a decision."

On the other hand, here's a situation where wisdom may enlist a little innocent and creative Shinola in a good cause. Wife to husband: "Does this dress make me look fat?" There is no need to put in print the obvious direct, blunt and less than loving responses. Sometimes speaking the truth in love can be done by speaking the truth in fun. A diplomatic, wise and loving answer might be, "Honey, we both put on a few pounds over the holidays because of your fabulous cooking, and fortunately for you, your natural pulchritude (beauty) eclipses your extraness."

* * *

Hear me right: a sound education is certainly of value. But always keep before you the examples of great wisdom.

It is widely agreed that Mother Teresa, the "Angel of Calcutta," who served the poorest and most invisible people her entire life, was a fountain of wisdom. Her shining character took her before kings, presidents, the rich, famous and most powerful people in the world. She was even honored with a Nobel Peace Prize. Mother Teresa spoke her heart and mind in a clear, compelling, and often daring way. For instance:

"Joy is a net of love by which you can catch souls."

"The hunger for love is much more difficult to remove than the hunger for bread."

"And today, [it is] unbelievable that the mother *herself* murders her own child, afraid of having to feed one more child, afraid to educate one more child. The child must die. This is one of the greatest poverties. A nation, people, family, that allows that, that accepts that, they are the poorest of the poor. "

(from her 1982 commencement address at Harvard)

Did her wisdom come (derive) from a rich education, extensive study and advanced degrees from elite universities? No (negative). It came from the bounty of her heart and soul.

The fear of the Lord is the beginning of wisdom. Proverbs 9:10

CS Lewis, steeped in books, languages, literature and history, is considered highly (supremely) educated. And yet, the great (voluminous) body of his writings consistently points to sacred realities. Did his insight and wisdom come from a wealth (copiousness) of education or a richness of soul and spirit? Most would say, yes (affirmative), the condition of his spirit shaped his writing more than his education, though he would not have been C.S. Lewis without his vast (prodigious) education.

* * *

Here's the bottom line: You can have the entire alphabet after your name, BA, MA, PhD, MD, DDS, DUH, LMNOP, conferred on you by the great universities of the world, but if you lack clear insight into the true nature of the world (cosmos), people (homo sapiens) and the unseen (metaphysical) changeless (immutable) realities... you are simply an educated, but not enlightened jaw-flapper, whose brain trumps (arrogates) his soul.

Still and all, the choice, my dear ones, is not whether to listen just to your brain or only to your soul... God gave us both.

If you feed your brain and neglect your soul, you may fall prey to a sharper mind. If you feed your soul and neglect your brain, you may be swept away by a charming (charismatic) wolf in sheep's clothing. So, feed both brain and soul, head and heart. The brain observes, collects, analyzes, and organizes. The soul determines value and true north. Feed your brain on great ideas, accurate information, essential principles and solid logic. Feed your soul on helping and serving others, on beauty, art, great stories (literature), soulful music, and truth, especially the big T truths in scripture. Do both and you will grow in wisdom and your brain will benefit as well.

Brain and soul together can help you recognize the subtle and shallow sheen of Shinola. However, between a large soul and a large brain - lean toward living, loving and speaking from your soul, because a rich, sensitive and nimble soul is your best ally to detect the oily stench (redolence) of Shinola and the sweet aroma of the sacred.

By the way, my aromatic progeny, you clearly are the very best part of me. I can tell. My soul smells the sacred in you.

Love, Dad

Character vs. *Charisma*

Those are my principles, and if you don't like them...
well, I have others.

Groucho Marx

Charm is deceptive

Proverbs 31:30

My Princess and Princes,

I once saw the hit musical "Into the Woods" on Broadway. Act One portrays five fairytales in their traditional telling and endings. But in the Second Act, all hell breaks loose in each tale. One of the fairytales is Cinderella. You know the story. After the fancy ball at the castle, Prince Charming searches far and wide for her and rescues her from the evil stepmother. He makes Cinderella his queen and they live happily ever after.

But happy endings have gone out of vogue in modern culture and theatre. So, after intermission, you get the rest of the story according to the writers of "Into the Woods." Prince Charming reveals what a narcissist (alternate spelling, j-e-r-k) he is. He cheats on her and justifies his behavior to a shocked and heartbroken Cinderella with this line:

"After all, I was raised to be charming, not sincere."

Turns out Prince Charming was not a prince of a character.

Bummer for Cinderella. Reality bites. But better to live without delusions, right? Without the "fairytale" of someone actually being a reliable, committed, solid person of their word.

I'm not saying 'happy ever after' is easy in a world full of challenge, heartache, and tragedy. You know some of those stories, too. But counting on charisma to face what life can throw at us is like building a cardboard house in a hurricane. It just won't hold up.

Charisma relies on style. Character on substance. Charisma runs on persona and charm. Character is characterized by integrity and authenticity. So, beware. Slick Shinola peddlers make a living selling shiny promises, immediate gratification, and cardboard houses. (See the letter: Leader vs. Politician)

In the music business, like most careers, charisma is marketable. It's part of having "the whole package." Talent is great, but a persuasive, magnetic personality sells, too. I remember a T-shirt went around for a while about how to be successful in the music business:

Once you can fake sincerity you've got it made.

Pretty cynical, huh? I'm happy to say, I've run into more solid people than flimsy ones.

In fact, one of the best ways to nurture your own character is to go into the woods surrounded by people of solid character. People you admire, who set the bar high. People you want to be like. There's an old saying, "Do not be misled. Bad company corrupts good character." That comes from 1 Corinthians 15:33. The opposite is true, too. Good company inspires and nurtures good character.

Life is a group hike, as we like to say, but ultimately, the choice is yours. Decide now what true north is. Set your heart and mind in that direction. I believe you've done that. You know that God and his ways are true north. Every morning, remind yourself of the compass heading of your soul. In compromising situations, remind yourself again. When a Shinola peddler makes an attractive pitch to veer even slightly off true north, hopefully, you'll sense the con. And choose the high road.

I say, hopefully. We all fall short and fall prey to temptation. I have to admit, I've chosen some flimsy things, compromised, sometimes taken the low road. I've been fooled and fooled myself.

When we compromise our principles, fall, sin, the course correction to make is a reset. Something most Prince Charmings avoid. How is a reset done?

First, repent. That's not a word you hear much these days, but essential for a true course correction. Persist in the wrong direction and your character will be among the first casualties. The story of the prodigal son in Luke 15 is such a powerful example of a humbling and beautiful course correction. As the story goes, when the son finally "came to his senses" he did a one-eighty, repented, and headed for home where his father was waiting, looking down the road for his return with open heart and open arms.

Just look around. Prodigals are everywhere, captive to pride and their own wounds. Most play the victim. Some are militant, committed to their own compass heading, and trying to sell it as "freedom," the pursuit of happiness, or just living their own "truth."

Second. Own it. The misstep. The poor choice. The sin. There's another word being scrubbed out of fashion by verbal spin masters attempting to airbrush our broken nature with a thin coat of denial. Excuses, blame shifting, and justifying are just more brands of Shinola we often sell ourselves. Owning our crap takes humility, another hallmark of character.

And third, set your soul again on true north to avoid drift. You can do this at any point. But the sooner the better. And it means less heartache to mend. Sadly, lots of people who set out for true north, degree by degree drift away. (See the letter: Grace vs. Tolerance)

My very human offspring, everyone falls. None of us is immune to that. The old hymn, Come Thou Fount, speaks for all of us.

> Prone to wander, Lord I feel it
> Prone to leave the God I love
> Here's my heart, oh take and seal it
> Seal it for Thy courts above

Resetting, getting back up, takes and creates, you guessed it, character. And more. Scripture says, "Suffering produces endurance; endurance, character; and character, hope." (Romans 5:3,4) Imagine that. Our character, tested and tried, can give us and others hope. Real hope. (See the letter: Hope vs. Optimism)

The opposite of compromise is character.

Frederick Douglas said that. He was born a slave in 1818. He learned to read in secret, rose to become the first black US Marshall, an author, and one of the most influential voices to end slavery in the US. His character gave hope to millions and helped changed the world.

My blessings, you have not been raised to be merely charming, fickle, or shallow. You have been raised to know true north, to be kind, honest, authentic, thoughtful and caring of those around you. (See the letter: Usie vs. Selfie)

Every day, two roads lead into the woods. The wide one – taken by those often lured in by flimsy but clever posers. The other road is less traveled - where the rebar of character is forged day by day. Choice by choice.

I see character growing in you. Through heartaches and stumbles, faith and pressing on, I see you getting stronger and shining brighter. That makes this dad's heart very glad.

Let me make sure you know this. The woods out there can be dark and deep. Situations and people can throw any of us off course. Should that happen, I am here. Praying for you. Looking down the road for you. With open heart and open arms.

Love, Dad

Letter 16

Leader vs. *Politician*

If your actions inspire others to dream more, learn more,
do more, and become more, you are a leader.

John Quincy Adams

Politicians are like diapers. They both need changing regularly,
and for the same reason.

Mark Twain

My inspirations,

You are never too young to understand and spot the difference between a politician and a leader. This will help you avoid one and become the other.

When it comes to Shinola, no one spreads it around more than politicians. They flap their jaws for a living and give street gangs strong competition for the bravado award. (see the letter: Bravado vs. Courage) There is no shortage of politicians. But true leaders may be an endangered species.

You are also not too young to decide which you will become. Already, every day, you have begun practicing the qualities to become either. Like a politician you can give me excuses why you haven't brushed your teeth or done your homework or just tell me the straight truth - you got too distracted by something (like a video game, but reading a book might play in your favor). Becoming a leader starts now.

Nothing so conclusively proves a man's ability to lead others
as what he does from day to day to lead himself.

Thomas J. Watson Sr. CEO of IBM

Sometimes when I drop you off at school in the morning what do I say? "Now get out there and lead someone!" Nope. I say, "Be awesome. Be kind. You can't be awesome if you can't be kind." (See Letter 9: Kind vs. Nice) Why? For several reasons. First, because God extends kindness to us. In fact, scripture says that his kindness leads us back to him. (Rom 2:4) God deals with us out of the "kind intention of his will." (Eph 1:5) God leads with kindness. That's a relief, right?

Leaders are kind. Politicians try to be nice - even when they're calling another politician a liar without using the word 'liar'. They use words like "misspoke," "mistaken" and "fact-challenged." Their five-dollar word is "disingenuous." That's an educated, polite way of calling someone a liar.

So why be kind in particular? Because people matter. Because character matters. (See the letter: Character vs. Charisma) And because good and great leaders care and influence people not primarily through ideas, promises, talent, vocabulary or intelligence, but through genuine character made real through action. John Quincy Adams didn't say, "If your *words* inspire". He said, "If your *actions* inspire."

These days lots of people are wowed by fancy talk, promises and talent. Knowing this, politicians become very skilled at speech making, public relations, marketing and disguising what they are really up to.

The magician and the politician have much in common: they both have to draw our attention away from what they are really doing.

Ben Okri- Nigerian poet/author

So, being a leader, someone not easily swayed by peer pressure, begins with character in action, not by impressive jaw-flapping.

Example is not the main thing in influencing others,
it is the only thing.

Albert Schweitzer

Another way to tell a politician from a leader is this. Politicians are pleasers. They don't want to upset people - at least 51 percent of the people - just enough to keep getting elected. Politicians tend to take their direction from polls, from what people think of them. On the other hand, leaders are servers. They take their main direction from principles to determine what will best serve and represent the people. Politicians sometimes even adjust their clothes or accent to the people they are with at the moment, seeking to relate and be accepted. (See the letter: Admiration vs. Popularity) Leaders remain true to themselves in different situations and are willing to take the heat for speaking the hard truth.

I cannot give you the formula for success, but I can give you the formula for failure, which is: Try to please everybody.

Herbert B. Swope
Winner of three Pulitzer Prizes in journalism

Let me give you a real-world example of great leadership.

As kids, so far I have never seen you take much interest in the yearly State of the Union address by our presidents. I don't blame you. It's pretty dry, predictable stuff. The speech is almost always a steady stream of jaw-flapping with pauses, mostly scripted, for his supporters to stand and applaud and rah-rah while the opposing side remains seated to express their resistance and irritation that their guy is not the President - yet. Their speeches are basically all the same: "Whatever is broken, it's because of my predecessor and I am doing a great job fixing his messes." Whether it's a broken economy, failing schools, unresolved wars, a hole in the ozone, a border crisis or whatever, "I have the power to fix it and I will." Most of the time, there is more "I" will fix it than "We" will fix it. "I" intend. "I" will bring change. "I" did this. "I" will do that. "We (meaning 'I') will prevail." Blah-Blah-Blah. The heavy use of the word "I" is a tipoff.

> The leaders who work most effectively, it seems to me, never say 'I.' And that's not because they have trained themselves not to say 'I.' They don't think 'I.' They think 'we'; they think 'team.' They understand their job to be to make the team function. They accept responsibility and don't sidestep it, but 'we' gets the credit. This is what creates trust, what enables you to get the task done.
>
> Peter Drucker – writer/economist

In these annual speeches, there is a lot of verbal bravado masquerading as courage, but no real courage on display. (See the letter: Courage vs. Bravado) The words and emotions are carefully paced and packed with fervor and alibis but very little raw, holy passion and truth. Maybe that's why so few people tune in to listen anymore. However, there was a State of the Union address that actually took real leadership to deliver.

Once upon a time on the other side of the globe, some years before you arrived on this beautiful, broken planet, a part of the world was waking up and getting free from a long night of a tyranny called communism. It was an idea crafted in the dark halls of power by Godless control freaks who thought making the rules for everyone else was an appealing job, especially since the rule makers didn't have to live by those rules themselves. It also paid well because the rule makers lived large off the treasury supplied by labor of the rule keepers.

New Year's Day 1990, Vaclav Havel, the newly elected President of free Czechoslovakia, delivered an address to the Czech people and the world. He spoke calmly, with great conviction, humility, honesty and courage. There were still many people who wanted power and would take it by force if given the chance. Havel knew this. Under the communist rulers, he had spent some years in prison for his views. Certainly, many of his former captors were listening to their former prisoner's speech.

On this great day, he spoke as the freed leader of a free people. Unlike most of our politicians, he spoke the naked truth. He basically said: Our country is broken, and we are the reason. He began by listing the lies of the previous political rulers saying, "I assume you did not propose me for this office so that I, too, would lie to you?" What an eloquent remark to connect with his supporters and simultaneously slam the previous tyrants. Brilliant. And courageous.

He followed that with the hard truth. You can find and read his entire speech for yourself, (I urge you to do that someday soon) but let me include a little of it here so you can hear what a real leader sounds like. Use it like a measuring stick to spot the Sacred, real thing or a shifty, Shinola peddling politician.

Early in his remarks, Havel got right to the point:

"The worst thing is that we live in a contaminated
moral environment."

I can't imagine any of our current politicians saying that - in public, on camera. He went on:

"We fell morally ill because we became used to saying
something different from what we thought. We learned not
to believe in anything, to ignore one another, to care only
about ourselves. Concepts such as love, friendship,
compassion, humility or forgiveness lost their depth and
dimension...

When I talk about the contaminated moral atmosphere... I
am talking about all of us... we are all... responsible... We
are all also its co-creators. We have to accept this legacy as a
sin we committed against ourselves. Freedom and democracy
include participation and therefore responsibility from us
all... If we realize this, hope will return to our hearts. "

Feel the awe in that? The courage, honesty and humility? Our politicians never take the blame for anything! They always point the finger at someone else. There are less than a handful of our current politicians who risk being this honest or expressing their spiritual faith in public as Havel went on to do.

"Our first president wrote: 'Jesus, not Caesar.' I dare to say that we may even have an opportunity to spread this idea further... Our country... can now permanently radiate love, understanding, the power of the spirit and of ideas."

Near the end of his speech, Havel even had something to say about jaw flapping.

"In conclusion, I would like to say that I want to be a President who will speak less and work more. To be a president who... will always be present among his fellow citizens and listen to them well."

Extraordinary, right? Did you notice how he said "we" a lot more than "I"? He described and set a new course for his country that day. But he had been heading in that direction with his life for many years. Whenever you hear words like Havel's, spoken fearlessly and backed up by a life of action, pray to be such a person.

Not the cry, but the flight of a wild duck, leads the
fluck to fly and follow.

Chinese Proverb

Here's another difference between politicians and leaders.

Politicians operate from a crafted and even crafty strategy driven by a distorted, self-serving view of the world. They take care to arrange everything for perception, how it looks and feels, in order to impress and convince those easily swayed by dramatics or hooked by promises. (This applies to people in general, too, not just those in public office. They're called "posers." They leave an aftertaste like most artificial sweeteners.)

Leaders speak and act from heartfelt conviction and a clear, realistic view of the world. They are more concerned about what is true, right and best than whether people and voters like them or what result it will have in the polls. (This is admirable in non-political people, too. They're called "authentic", "real", or "true-blue" and they make the best friends, spouses and partners in business and ministry.)

"A man who wants to lead the orchestra must turn
his back on the crowd." Aristotle – author

Vaclav Havel's speech was not delivered to a massive crowd for maximum dramatic effect. Politicians often carefully stage and events to produce cheers and photos. Even though Havel was a playwright and poet and knew how to move a crowd, he didn't pose in a dramatic setting, artfully lit and produced by filmmakers. Instead, he delivered those potent words seated behind a desk through a camera into the homes of the people.

Courage, a prime trait of great leaders, unlike bravado, produces honor, admiration and even tears. I am sure there were all three in homes all across Czechoslovakia that New Year's day.

* * *

Now let me give you an example much closer to home, in fact from our own home.

Wyatt, I will never forget the evening you wrestled with the decision whether to move up to the A-team in soccer, or remain with the guys you had played with for two years. You were a captain on the B-team. Your team was becoming a strong unit and had just come off a big victory at a tournament against teams in higher divisions. The next week, right after tryouts, remember, the A-team coach came to us and said he wanted you on his team. In his view, you were ready. But the choice was up to you.

This was a tough decision. We had to call the coach that evening or lose the slot. You and your mom and I went over and over all the pros and cons. The A-team meant starting over, with new teammates, higher skill levels. It probably meant less playing time, not being captain and a lot of hard work to improve and prove yourself all over again. You were very anxious about taking that big a step. The A-team was actually up four division levels! There was the added pressure of letting both teams down, leaving one and possibly not measuring up sometimes on the other. The tension was real.

Your mom lobbied hard for you to join the A-team. I leaned that way, too, but also saw the benefits of playing one more year with the B-team and your buddies, being a leader, and one of the top players. I told you I would support either choice. We left the decision in your hands.

Just when I thought you were leaning toward the safer choice, the B-team, you grinned and said, "Ok, I want to join the A-team."

I can't describe the rush of admiration that went through me. I feel it again now as I write this, and I remember the joy on your face once you spoke your choice out loud. We got the coach on the phone. I told him you had made a decision and handed the phone to you.

Your face beamed as you told him, "Coach, I want to be on your team."

I felt like you had just signed with a professional team for millions of dollars! Your mom and I were so proud of you. We still are, for a lot of reasons.

If you do not choose to lead, you will forever be led by others.
Find what scares you, and do it. And you can
make a difference.
J. Michael Straczynski – TV producer

In that moment, in the heat of decision making, where two roads led into the future and you could only choose one, Wyatt, you took a pivotal step toward becoming a leader. You chose the difficult, more challenging path. And in our home, your decision produced honor, admiration, tears - and cheers.

Now get out there, my lovely world changers, run, play ball, serve, live what you speak, fly high and true - and be awesome. Be kind. You can't be awesome if you can't be kind.

Love, Dad

Blessed vs. *Lucky*

Luck is not the hand of God.

Kurt Vonnegut – author

My blessings,

Strange but true, some people carry a rabbit's foot in their pocket, hoping it will bring them good luck. I never understood this. It obviously didn't work for the rabbit, and it had four.

So-called "lucky" objects come in a great variety. Four-leaf clovers, lucky pennies, horseshoes, hats, even a wishbone from a chicken. Chain letters used to circulate, requiring the recipient to pass it along or risk bad luck by breaking the chain. Some people count on their "lucky" stars and consult a daily horoscope to guide their decisions. Sailors once believed seeing a dolphin upon leaving port was a good omen for the voyage. Obviously, the crew of the Titanic didn't spot one leaving Queenstown port in Ireland in 1912.

Witchdoctors in primitive cultures call these supposed lucky items talismans. They believe and convince others some power resides in an object or event that can somehow sway the forces of the universe in their favor.

But you and me, we don't believe in luck.

Before one of your soccer matches or musical events or big tests at school, I never say, "Good luck." There's a reason for that.

Being blessed and counting on luck represent very different views of life. Is your storyline and mine just a cosmic slot machine of random tumblers that line up and pay off big for only the lucky few? Is the universe a system of forces that can be manipulated by crossing our fingers? Does the outcome of a soccer game or history test depend on luck? Or on how much you practice or study?

Blessed and lucky reflect vastly different states of mind and heart. A sense of being blessed comes from trusting something larger and more personal than the physical, insentient (unfeeling and unthinking) universe. Blessing is usually marked by gratitude. Leaning on luck is a mixed drink of positive vibes and desperation, usually marked by hype and frustration, ending in a pity party. "This could be my lucky day." "Dang, I never win!" "What am I, invisible to the odds gods?" (See the letter: Hope vs. Optimism)

> Luck is merely an illusion,
> trusted by the ignorant, chased by the foolish.
> Timothy Zahn – Science Fiction author

Believing in being blessed over being lucky, do I occasionally buy a lottery ticket? (at Sawyer's suggestion.) And play the 300 million to one odds? Yes, especially when the total rises to hundreds of millions. I sometimes wonder if buying one is a lack of faith in God to provide, or an act of faith to give him another avenue to bless me. Ha! And like every other lottery ticket holder, I've played the mental game, "What If?" So far, the "force" has not been with me. At least not in that way. (See the letter: Faith vs. Fate)

Here's the primary reason we don't rely on the fickle factor of luck.

Jesus never said, "Good luck, ya'll," or, "Yikes, I didn't see that coming." Imagine how absurd. If he had, that would mean he was just like the rest of us, oblivious to the future and constantly blindsided by the uncertain nature of life. But of course, the Lord had an advantage. He knew there was a plan. He was in on the plan. And he was the plan.

It's our nature to want to know what's over the horizon, which way to go, what the stock market will do, how the game is going to turn out. Why do you think there are so many time travel stories and movies? Some of our favorites: Back to the Future, Frequency, Time Bandits and Ground Hog Day. In all of them, someone capitalizes on knowing what's going to happen. If that were possible, who needs faith or luck, right?

Likewise, in the Beatitudes, Jesus didn't say: Lucky are the meek. Lucky are the merciful, those who mourn, the peacemakers and the pure in heart. He called them "blessed."

Here's a better "What If" game. What if we can be blessed, no matter what happens? Come what may? In better times or worse. Come joy or sorrow. In sickness and health. Richer or poorer. Blessed actually means "filled" or "satisfied," in the favor of and in tune with the will of God.

Doesn't that sound a lot better than being lucky?

Not so strange, but true, I actually won a lottery of sorts. The genetic lottery. Not via a random convergence of chromosomes. But by a bigger plan. Psalm 139 says the days ordained for us were written in God's book before any of them came to be. Every one of us was thought of, planned for, ahead of time. God saw us coming. No pregnancies were ever unexpected to him. No lucky stars determined our destinies. No rabbit's foot influenced our futures.

Our Heavenly Father came right out and revealed what was ahead,

> I know the plans I have for you… to give you a future
> and a hope.
>
> God, in Jeremiah 29:11

You, my blessings, are my winning lottery tickets. My cup is filled and runneth over. I am blessed, not lucky, to be your father.

Love, Dad

Letter 18

Prayer vs. *Vibes*

All those who believe in psychokinesis - raise my hand.

Stephen Wright – comedian

My bagel-loving believers,

Psychokinesis or telekinesis is an imagined ability to move objects or make things happen from a distance by mental power alone. Wouldn't that be nice? No more, "Please, pass the butter," or "I wish this traffic would clear." The only documented case of psychokinesis is what Jesus could do. He filled the disciples' nets (plural) with fish, made a fig tree wither, put a gold coin in a fish's mouth, and healed people - all from a distance. He even knew people's thoughts, personal histories and future events.

But in our hands, the power of telekinesis would probably end like an episode of the Twilight Zone sarcastically called, "It's a Good Life." (season 3, episode 8) Remember that one? A six-year-old, undisciplined brat, Anthony, has godlike mental powers, including mind-reading. Everyone in town is terrified of him, so they tell him everything he does is good. Hence the title of the episode. His tyranny is absolute. He punishes unhappy or critical thoughts, brutally murdering any resistors by casting them into a cornfield. He even turns one man into a jack-in-the-box with his head bouncing on a spring. Anthony definitely did not give off good vibes.

These days, there's a seemingly harmless echo of the notion of telekinesis. From more and more people, especially news anchors and public figures, you'll hear, "Our thoughts are with you." Or "We're sending good thoughts." The cool version is, "Sending good vibes your way." Those are nice sentiments. (See the chapter Kind vs. Nice) They show care. The world can sure use more of that. But those expressions can also be polite, hollow mannerisms, merely a show of caring.

And when you pray, do not heap up empty phrases...

Matthew 5:6-8

To be fair, "I'm praying for you" can be a hollow mannerism, too. An empty phrase. Unless prayer actually happens for the person or situation.

I suspect I'm scribbling to my own small choir. Ever since you were little, we said our prayers at bedtime. We prayed before meals. When any of us was sick. In the driveway before heading out on trips. About big decisions. Your mom and I prayed for each of you before you were born. So, I'm pretty sure you know the difference between prayer and the cultural politeness of "good thoughts." But as a reminder, again, it's like two very different roads diverging into the world.

Whenever I read or hear someone express, "Our thoughts are with you," though I appreciate sincere empathy, it falls very short. Stephen Wright's humor makes the point obvious. "Raise my hand."

That's hilarious. But seriously, is there really any power in our thoughts to move or change something?

In the 1950s, a pastor, Norman Vincent Peale, wrote a book, *The Power of Positive Thinking*. It became a best seller. Basically, it promoted the idea that the root of success lies in the mind. That we can reshape our life by taking control of our thoughts and changing our attitude. And there's some merit in that. Scripture has a lot to say about renewing our minds and thinking about higher things. How we think definitely shapes us. (See the chapters Success vs. Significance and Dignity vs. Ego)

As a man thinks in his heart, so he is. Proverbs 23:7

But I'm not talking about that kind of thinking. I'm talking about the kind of casual, mirage mentality that thinks our thoughts hold some invisible, metaphysical power to mend a broken bone or heart, pass a test or make a sixty-foot putt go in the hole. Sending thoughts is actually far less effective than sending a Hallmark card.

Prayer, on the other hand, is a direct appeal to the God and Maker of the universe who has assured us he is listening.

This is the confidence we have in approaching God: that if we ask anything according to his will, he hears us. And if we know that he hears us, whatever we ask, we know that we have what we asked of him.

1 John 5:14,15

I wrestle with the last part of that because I've prayed for many things that didn't happen the way I asked. You have, too. I have to chalk that up to what I prayed was not in his will, or God is in control of the universe and I am clearly not. It's probably both. Even Jesus prayed a prayer that wasn't answered the way he asked. In the Garden of Gethsemane, facing the agony of his death he prayed, "Father, if possible let this cup pass from me." It didn't pass. He endured the cross. Maybe the way he ended that prayer is a good example for us when we pray. "Yet not mine, but thy will be done."

Another reality makes prayer trump good vibes. I've prayed for many things that have happened the way I asked. (Like having wonderful children someday.) But I can't think of anything out there in the real world that my "good thoughts" made happen. And yet, here's a mind blower. God "knows my thoughts from afar." (Psalm 139:2) Makes you think, huh? Hopefully, good thoughts. Ha!

Two examples of amazing prayers and then I'll put an 'amen' on this.

During the Revolutionary War, in the harsh winter of 1777, a Quaker named Potts happened upon George Washington praying alone in the woods. Pott's eyewitness account was recorded in a diary of Reverend Nathanial Snowden. Potts told Snowden what he saw and heard.

"I heard a plaintive sound as, of a man at prayer. I tied my horse to a sapling & went quietly into the woods & to my astonishment I saw the great George Washington on his knees alone, with his sword on one side and his cocked hat on the other. He was at Prayer to the God of the Armies,

beseeching to interpose with his Divine aid, as it was ye
Crisis, & the cause of the country, of humanity & of the world."

George Washington did not walk out in a wintry wood to send "good thoughts" to his men. He did what Jesus did. He withdrew to a solitary place and prayed fervently. (Other accounts say he did this often.) His prayer was basically, "God, help." God did. I have to assume a great number of British soldiers asked for God's help, too. History and scripture lead me to assume he answered them "according to his will."

Fast forward about fourscore years to Abraham Lincoln's prayer for the nation. Here's a portion of it.

"Almighty God… We humbly beseech Thee that we may always prove ourselves a people mindful of Thy favor and glad to do Thy will. Save us from violence, discord, and confusion, from pride and arrogance, and from every evil way. Defend our liberties, and fashion into one united people, the multitude brought hither out of many kindreds and tongues. Endow with Thy spirit of wisdom… that there may be justice and peace at home, and that through obedience to Thy law, we may show forth Thy praise among the nations of the earth. In time of prosperity fill our hearts with thankfulness, and in the day of trouble, suffer not our trust in Thee to fail; all of which we ask through Jesus Christ our Lord. Amen."

Is that powerful or what? But not surprising. Unlike more recent presidents (who shall go unnamed), Washington and Lincoln were not known for "empty phrases." They didn't just send charismatic, good vibes to the troops and the nation. They prayed. To God. Asking with gratitude. In fact, except for the style of language, Václav Havel, who I told you about in the letter Leader vs. Politician, strikes a lot of the same chords as Lincoln.

FYI: On July 4, 1952, President Truman began the National Day of Prayer. President Reagan moved it to the first Thursday in May. Thank God it has not simply become the National Day of Good Vibes. So far.

Clearly, the fundamental difference between prayer and sending "good vibes" is acknowledging the power source. Prayer is communication that believes Someone is listening. Someone who can change and make things happen beyond our ability or capacity. Good thoughts and vibes, aside from a kernel of good intention and empathy, are like an extension cord - not plugged into a wall socket or into the thing that needs electricity. Current cannot possibly flow from source to need. In prayer, source and need are connected. The current habit (see what I did there?) of sending "good thoughts" is very revealing about the drift in our world. A drift away from the power source.

My sacred saints in training, I've told you the two prayers you will likely pray most in your life. "Lord, help" and "Thank you, Lord." Often you will say them in the same prayer. One is a request. One is gratitude. This makes perfect sense. Scripture actually says:

Do not be anxious about anything, but in every situation, by prayer and petition, with thanksgiving, present your requests to God.

Philippians 4:6

I started praying for each of you long before you arrived. I've never stopped. And as long as I have breath, I will bring your names up often in my prayers. And probably even from a balcony in heaven after I graduate from here.

My answers to prayer, I pray you'll pray all your lives, and stay connected to the power source. Amen.

Love, Dad

Letter 19

Dignity vs. *Ego*

Til He appeared… and the soul felt it's worth.

John Sullivan Dwight
from "O Holy Night"

We can't all be stars because someone
has to sit on the curb and clap as I go by.

Sebastian Horsely - author

My royalty,

"I'm pretty bored these days." These words were spoken by a good friend in a group of guys that I met with for many years. We got together nearly every week to compare notes, encourage and support each other, pray and do life together.

On this particular day, one brilliant friend relayed his life as he reclined on the couch. He followed his comment about being bored with this: "That may be because my life is pretty self-involved." After a long pause, he capped it off with the cheerful proclamation: "Fortunately, I'm fascinating!" We erupted in laughter, including my eloquent friend.

His revelation was a perfect mix of honesty, innocence, playful ego and at the core - a rich vein of truth: that we spend far too many waking hours and deluded years being self-preoccupied. One of the Pied Pipers leading to the remote getaway called the Isle of Self, population 1, is Ego.

So, what is Ego? I'm glad you asked. Besides being a pretty handy scrabble word, Ego is like a Homeland Security (actually Insecurity) Department in our heads. It's the part of our conscious self that makes us self-conscious, always looking out for what others think of us and what we think of ourselves. Ego's mission can include the following:

– monitoring how attractive we look, how smart, competent or athletic we appear.

– defending and justifying our motives, intentions and actions.

– making sure we always have an answer or an impressive opinion about every topic. The fancy word for that is ultracrepidarian. Not a Scrabble-friendly word, and it almost sounds like a compliment. But it's not. Try it on your all-knowing friends. "You're a real ultracrepidarian." The worst Shinola peddlers tend to be ultracrepidarians, i.e., full of crap.

All of us have an ego. Some bigger than others. I love this clever, self-aware comment:

> As I was driving down Beach Blvd, I saw a building that
> said, "Self Storage," and I thought, I wonder if my ego could
> possibly fit in just one unit.
>
> Jarod Kintz - author

As a family, we spent years around soccer. Think about how Ego shows itself there. When you hear or say, "That guy's a ball hog. He never passes to anyone," Ego may be involved, right? Wyatt and Sawyer, think of the times you passed the ball to someone who is in a better position to score, even though you could have taken a shot. That's playing like a team, willing to make an assist, instead of always being the guy who takes the shot, gets the goal. In that selfless moment, you don't just practice good teamwork, you practice telling your Ego to sit on the bench and shut up. You resist its inner push for the spotlight, for the sake of the team.

Ego is constantly managing our image, making it line up with how we want to be seen. It tries to keep any flaws or cracks from showing, to avoid looking clumsy or stupid or not up to snuff in any situation. Ego never says, "I'm sorry." "I was wrong." "I can be an idiot." "Please forgive me."

To the contrary:

> The ego puts its own interest first and twists every
> argument, word, even fact, to suit that interest.
>
> Paul Brunton - author

Who does that sound like? Here's a hint. It sounds like "politician." (See the letter: Leader vs. Politician)

To be honest, all of us can spin reality, become our own PR department.

Whenever you hear that little voice inside trying to sound bigger than it is, telling you things like, *I'm not that bad, I deserve good things to happen, They just don't understand, It wasn't my fault,* your ego has at least one hand on the steering wheel. That voice can get louder and angrier and say things like, *I'll never put myself in that position again! I'll show them! I am done trying!* At that point, Ego is white-knuckling the wheel with both hands; you have exited the freeway to growth and are being driven down Fear Avenue to an ugly town called Bitterville.

How do I know? Truth be told, I have traveled that road and eaten alone at a table for one in the Diner of Disappointment. Trust me, the only thing worse than the cold food is the service. The staff is irritable and too busy explaining why they shouldn't be there.

Ego rarely sleeps. It is vigilant. 24/7 it has one job: constantly prop up your persona, the mask or false self you present to the world. Sounds exhausting, right? The Persian poet Rumi called Ego the "veil between humans and God."

So, what motivates Ego? I'll give you three guesses. (A) fear, (B) insecurity, (C) vanity. If you wish there was another option, (D) all of the above, your instinct is correct. But something else lies below these. Fear of what? An insecurity about something hidden? A vanity to conceal and deflect from a deficit of some kind? No one wants to feel less than or exposed.

Day by day, the show goes on. We act brave when we're scared. (See the letter: Courage vs. Bravado) We appear confident when we're actually very uncertain inside. We hide behind the designer fig leaf of vanity. As a result, we only see each other dressed in the distortions and layers carefully managed and presented by our egos.

The famous playwright, Tennessee Williams, said this masquerade clouds all our relationships, except, and get this. Hear this. Monitor how his words affect you. Williams said this guardedness in relationships is the human norm *except*, except in the

"rare case of two people who love intensely enough to burn
through all those layers of opacity (lack of transparency)
and see each other's naked hearts."

Wow! When I first read that something in me said, "I want to love
and be loved like that!" Who doesn't want that? Deep down. (See
the letter: True Love vs. Infatuation)

Isn't that beautiful? Wonderful? But scary, right?

Why scary? Because what lies beneath our fear, insecurity and
vanity is a core doubt about our worth. What if somebody really
saw our naked heart? And rejects us? Big OUCH. Been there. How
do you risk that again, right? Is it any wonder we hide behind Ego,
instead of living from our Dignity? It's a lot safer. But living masked
is settling for less than being fully alive. Groucho Marx said,

"Blessed are the cracked, for they shall let in the light."

Isn't that delightful and insightful? Perhaps even better: blessed
are the transparent, for they will let in love.

The obvious question, my royal offspring, is this: What
determines our worth? Gives us dignity. How beautiful and
attractive I am? How talented? How stuffed my bank account?
The color of my skin? The pedigree of my ancestors? What binds
and gags our Ego so we can see and hear who we truly are?

The Declaration of Independence (I know. Again with the
founders' document, right? How many times will I refer to that? I

can't help that it holds such foundational truths.), the Declaration points to the source of our dignity. "Created equal…endowed by their Creator." "Modern" or "enlightened" culture is intent on severing that Divine tie.

Case in point.

The 1970s (you've seen pictures of my long hair and VW bus) was a decade of classic rock music, bell-bottoms, and tie-dye until it surrendered to Disco, polyester and drum machines. In that decade, a lot of college students hung a poster on their dorm room wall: The Desiderata. You can easily find a copy of it. It was written in 1927 by Max Erhmann, an attorney and hobby poet from Indiana. The word desiderata is Latin, meaning "things we want or need." Of course, we want and need some things listed in Erhmann's declaration: peace with our self and others, to enjoy our work, discernment, be comfortable in our own skin, affection, strength to face hardships, a sense of purpose about life. Some bits of his poem even paraphrase Biblical passages, but it diverges into an entirely different worldview.

Forty years after it was penned, the Desiderata became a hippie creed for living a groovy alternative to the ten commandments and the love chapter, Corinthians 13. It offered a baker's dozen of softly worded suggestions. "Go placidly amid the noise and the haste." "Be yourself." "Be cheerful." "Be happy." Not only hippies, but all kinds of people got on board seeking peace and wearing peace signs through the haze of cannabis, harder drugs and prescription medicine. Not much has changed.

I've told you about the half dozen times in my early twenties I tried marijuana. It only made me cough and gave me headaches.

Probably a providential bummer. I didn't see the attraction, besides getting free room and meals in jail back then. Without weed, at least I could face the fog of my selfishness without the smoke cloud of cannabis obscuring the real issues, which enabled a huge portion of my generation to put off growing up.

A sociologist called that a "psychosocial moratorium." Fancy term, huh? Sounds like what a lot of people like me studied in college trying to avoid the Vietnam war. Who can blame them? I don't. My high draft lottery number and scoliosis kept me from that war. Otherwise, I might have fled to Canada like some did, and you might have grown up playing hockey instead of soccer and replacing every question mark in a conversation with "Eh."

Two of the Desiderata's maxims went viral, or more accurately, spread like a virus through the twentieth and into the twenty-first century. The virus is alive and well. "Speak your truth" became the mantra freeing the individual from capital T, Truth. (See the letter: Truth vs. Ruse) The ancient wisdom spoken by Jesus, "You Shall know the Truth and the Truth shall set you free," went out of style. How liberating to determine your own truth, right? And follow the one infallible guiding North star at the center of your universe – you.

Speak or live your own truth is not new advice. Fathers have been giving their children this advice long before Andy Griffith passed his wisdom along to Opie.

In Shakespeare's play, Hamlet, a father, Polonius, gives his son Laertes advice as he heads off to the university. He tells his son, "To thine own self be true." That sounds noble and good, right? Almost biblical, like Solomon said it. But he didn't. Solomon had quite different advice in Ecclesiastes. Basically, fear God, keep his commands and enjoy the work of your hands. And in his fading years, he emphasized, everything else is meaningless. Sounds like one of the original bummers, huh? Ecclesiastes sure doesn't make a crowd do the wave these days.

For some time now, the view that there is objective, absolute, God-centered Truth has not only been discarded, but reviled. More on why and how that relates to our dignity in a moment.

Hit musicals and movies have been written about speaking your own truth and being true to yourself. It puts meat in the seats. Makes bank. Why? Ego laps it up. Look what I did. Look how I beat the odds. I stood against all norms against traditions and outdated notions. As Sinatra sang, "I did it my way." (See the letters: Usie vs. Selfie and Courage vs. Bravado)

A second maxim in the Desiderata created a loophole in theology big enough to drive the planet through: "Be at peace with God, *whatever you conceive Him to be.*" Create God in your own imagination is the new religion. Well, again, not that new. Cultures have been at that long before the Israelites forged a golden calf and bowed down to it.

Imagine me telling you as you head out into the world, "My sons, my daughter, get out there and find a god in the marketplace of gods that suits you, fits your style. One that gives you the confidence to go through life being true primarily to yourself, and don't let anyone else's god or truth deter you. Be yourself. Live your truth. Have a nice day and life."

Look around, my wing-growing fledglings, isn't that everywhere? And the chaos from it grows. These days, going "placidly" into the noise and the haste of the world requires all the supplements, pills, weed, booze, psychedelic concoctions and stress-relieving potions late night TV Shinola peddlers and dispensaries have to offer.

But wait. There's more!

Perhaps the shiniest Shinola in the Desiderata is this sales pitch. It blends a big T Truth with a silver-tongued, poetic view of our place in the cosmos.

> "You are a child of the universe
> no less than the trees and the stars;
> You have a right to be here."

Big T Truth in that? Yes, in a true sense, we have a right to be here. More accurately, a destiny. (See the letter: Significance vs. Success) Our founders stated this in the Declaration. One of our rights, granted by our Creator, is life. Psalm 139 predates their affirmation by about twenty-five-hundred years. God knits us together, "fearfully and wonderfully," in our mother's womb. That's big T Truth. Not just King David's personal truth.

The Desiderata, however, takes the view that we are each a "child of the universe." Not a child of big G God. Do you think there's any chance Darwin influenced Erhmann's view on that at all? Likely.

(BTW. If Darwin's brand of evolution actually has veracity, I've always wondered why we didn't keep our prehensile tail. You know, the one some monkeys still use to grab tree limbs? Just think, you could hold a beer, a taco, and still keep one arm around your babe!)

Whether or not Darwin influenced the amateur poet, the language of the Desiderata implies that lifeless matter, the universe, somehow "decided" to have children. You'd think on pure logical grounds that would be a hard sell. But people buy it. Hook, line and self-worth sinker.

The real sinker is in the middle assertion, regarding our value. Look at it. Our worth in the universe is "no less than the trees and the stars." So, trees are children of the universe as well? And stars, too? Granted, the author employed poetic license, stretching the meaning of words for artistic purpose. But words have meaning, and Shinola peddlers are notoriously clever word and reality shifters.

By the way, the writers of the Bible used poetic language, too. A lot. Look at this:

> The heavens declare the glory of God;
> the skies proclaim the work of his hands.
> Day after day they pour forth speech;
> night after night they reveal knowledge.
> They have no speech, they use no words;
> no sound is heard from them.
> Yet their voice goes out into all the earth,
> their words to the ends of the world.
>
> Psalm 19:1-4

Here's the difference. The Psalmist clearly states the universe does not actually speak words. Creation is evidence pointing to God, the Creator of the universe, not to itself as a living thing. The universe cannot give life or endow rights. Our origin and destinies are not created by or written in the stars. Still, millions of people pay subscriptions to horoscopes and big bucks to astrology readers. I once met a lady on a flight back from Europe who attended a convention of "ancestry and destiny readers." She was excited to learn in past lives she had been Joan of Arc and Anne Frank! And it only cost her $10,000! What a bargain, right? I wondered if the more you paid, the more famous your ancestry was.

Shinola peddlers do a verbal sleight of hand with language. Their pitch goes just like the Hobo to Opie: Question accepted views; plant seeds of doubt; then close with the offer of a shiny new, liberating perception. Sound familiar? Like another story about a garden and a snake? That Genesis story included the original Shinola peddler.

To be fair, Ehrmann probably set out just to write an encouraging free verse poem. And here I am picking his bones a hundred years later as one source of a dignity-eating virus. He also did not write the poem as advice to his children. He never had children. One of his diary entries reveals why he wrote it. "I should like, if I could, to leave a humble gift - a bit of chaste prose that had caught up some noble moods." Not sure what he meant by "chaste," which normally means sexually pure. Can you smell a hint of ego in there, endorsing his own writing as pure and above reproach?

Whatever his state of mind and faith, he drifted into a buffet of "whatever-floats-your-boat" philosophy of practical suggestions and Hallmark card sentiments. It was philosophy, not theology, because there was no big G God in Ehrmann's universe. But the

Shinola shoe fits him and fits even better on the crafty peddlers since then who blended his poem into the recipe of the Shinola pushed day and night today.

Ehrmann could not have foreseen that his "chaste prose" and "noble moods" either strayed or were steered into the murky waters of what would become New Age-Progressive-Hippy think. He provided sequins for another colorful Marti Gras mask to hide behind, to believe and do whatever you want to believe or do, without the pesky nuisance of morality, integrity and reality. (See the letter: Character vs. Charisma)

During the same period, over the pond in England, Aldus Huxley authored the futuristic novel "Brave New World" (which I strongly encourage you to read). He freely admitted he and his atheist cronies threw off big G God and religion for personal liberty, in particular for sexual freedom of expression. The sexual revolution of the sixties was far from new.

Don't misunderstand, like the author of the Desiderata, I love trees and stars. Early on, you guys loved to climb them, especially you, Wyatt. We loved to look at the stars, outside or through the skylight in the secret room I built you. (Sawyer, you were too young to get in on that.) Apparently, Mr. Ehrmann admired stars, too. But have no doubt, I place your value much higher than trees and stars. Though the attorney turned poet never had children of his own, I would bet my favorite tacos that if pressed, he valued his nieces and nephews more than the trees in his yard. And the stars in the sky.

Would it surprise you to know Mr. Ehrmann was a devout Christian in his youth? But by the time he wrote the poem at age fifty-five, he admitted he became "disillusioned" with orthodox Christianity. That happens a lot. The complexities of life and rapid shift of cultural norms can make the original fires of faith burn low. Faith can cool and drift. Sometimes die out completely, and become another victim of a steady diet of Shinola, resulting in a hardening of the heart and soul.

In particular, Max's "child of the universe" pitch got legs in the culture. People developed a taste for that Shinola and a crapload more. Sacred became a harder sell.

The difference is still glaringly obvious.

IF there is no big G God, a Creator, who made us in His image, and instead, thoughtless and lifeless matter simply "willed" its way out of the primordial ooze into complex critters who build and play guitars, create computer code, do standup comedy and write poetry about the universe "birthing" us - then life is just a Darwinian-Freudian grudge match: the fittest, biggest, strongest egos win. And the majority of us will sit on the curb and clap as the biggest posers parade by. As for our worth, our dignity, according to Ehrmann it could be "no more than the [thoughtless] trees and the [lifeless] stars."

Trees die. Fall. Turn into dirt. So do we. Stars burn out unnoticed in the immense void of space. If being human is no more than that, the faith of America's founders and their declaration were futile and misguided - Psalm 19 is just a fanciful view of a dead cosmos - and Psalm 139 is a folktale from a flawed man and songwriter desperate for meaning, identity and an unfailing Father figure. End of story.

IF, on the other hand, we are fearfully and wonderfully made by a big G God, in his likeness, who endowed us with big D Divine rights, who himself came from an eternal realm, became like us, starting as a helpless baby, grew into a man, suffered and sacrificed himself for the broken condition of the souls he gave us, then... then, though we may be unworthy of that sacrifice, we are not worthless! We are children of God. He, not the universe, is our Father. We have royal roots. Dignity. And an eternal destiny.

My treasures, living a self-involved, ego-driven life leads to boredom, emptiness and loneliness. I hope those who choose that road enjoying playing by themselves. (See the letter: Usie vs. Selfie)

In stark contrast, living from dignity enables you to be your true self - comfortable in your skin, warts, cracks, sins and all. (And someday wrinkles and bifocals.) Dignity enables us to recognize and honor it in others. To connect and care.

So, beware, my discerning descendants, of persuasive Pied Pipers selling "noble moods" drenched in poetic potions promising peace and unity, proclaiming all truths and all little 'g' gods can get along and fit on the same bumper sticker. (See the letter: Grace vs. Tolerance) I pray you learn to spot them. You shall know them by their Shinola.

A current horde of high-tech, high-functioning Shinola peddlers shun and absolutely denounce absolute big 'T' Truth, and big 'C' Christianity. (See the letter: Heaven vs. Sky) Most of this brand of charlatan have dispensed with subtlety. Why? Hubris. That's from the Greek, meaning pride. One of its most potent incarnations is Ego, that silver-tongued hijacker none of us is completely rid of in this life.

So, my shining stars, in the face of it all, live maskless.

Transparent. Easy? No. How? As a general rule, feed the ego, starve the soul. Feed the soul, starve the ego. Here's a reliable key. A strong antidote to Ego and Hubris is - humility. It comes from being secure in the source of our dignity, knowing our Maker and Remaker has determined our worth, even fully aware of our warts and cracks.

The writer of "O, Holy Night" got it right.

> Long lay the world in sin and error pining
> Til He appeared... and the soul felt it's worth.

My children, you are valuable. Beyond measure. As your Dad, I am biased, of course. But a reliable big S Source tells me it's so.

Love, Dad

Letter 20

Forgiveness vs. *Apology*

Forgiveness is the fragrance that the violet sheds
on the heel that has crushed it.

Mark Twain

My fragrant blossoms,

Wyatt, one of my early sins against you still hurts my heart when I think about it. You may not remember this. I hope your heart doesn't. You were about four years old. We left the house together in my car. You were in the back seat. Just after we pulled out of the driveway, your seatbelt came undone. I was in a hurry and irritated about something, so, of course, it didn't occur to me that I probably didn't push the buckle in all the way. I kept driving, turned around and tried to tell you how to fasten it. You struggled with it and couldn't plug it back in. Not wanting to stop and fasten it myself, I said something demeaning like, "Come on! It's not rocket science!" You started crying. The look on your face stabbed me to the core. I knew immediately I had crushed your spirit. Wounded the heart of my beautiful little boy. What a horrible feeling. I pulled over, came around to your side, opened the door, got down on my knees and said how sorry I was. I'll never forget how you turned your face away from me and kept crying. It still makes me tear up just describing it. An apology was not enough.

My behavior was not a mistake. It was sinful. I held you and kept asking you to forgive me. You did. But even now, it reminds me what my heart is capable of.

I think I mentioned him before. The English poet, Alexander Pope, wrote, "To err is human, to forgive divine." We generally think of erring as making a mistake, an error, an oops. Well, I am definitely human. That kind of erring comes easy.

The word comes from a Latin verb meaning to stray or wander. I'm not sure if Pope lumped mistakes and sin together. In his time, the 1700s, err probably covered both. But by connecting err with forgiveness, he seems to imply the more serious infraction. I'm sure you know which one that is. As a human, I do. Making mistakes and sinning both come easy for me.

Newsflash: your dad is a sinner.

Here's what I'm getting at: Mistakes usually only need an apology. Sin requires forgiveness.

These days, most people believe we humans are basically good.

When I was a teenager, a pop psychiatrist wrote a book called, "*I'm OK. You're Ok.*" It sold like crazy. It expressed a truth, but told less than the whole truth. Its central theme was: "Every human being is of value, important and to be taken into full account." True. Certainly true. But it didn't take into account that some of our actions and thoughts are a long way from OK. In a culture eager to take the path of least resistance, his slogan became a banner for the basic goodness of human nature. The conscience-easing idea that nobody's perfect and everyone is OK, virtually replaced, "All have sinned and fallen short of the glory of God." (Romans 3:23)

Quite a while back, a character on the show Saturday Night

Live mocked this pop psychology. His episodes are hysterical. You can find them. Stuart Smalley, a "caring nurturer" but not a licensed therapist, hosted a talk show called "Daily Affirmations." He attempted to help people, basically affirming every guest and nearly everything they do and feel with, "And that's OK." (See the letter: Grace vs. Tolerance) At the beginning and end of every sketch, Stuart recited his slogan into a mirror, "I'm good enough. I'm smart enough. And doggone it, people like me."

My children, you are plenty smart enough to know that if people are basically good and OK, why the heck is the world so full of fussing and fighting, broken relationships, wickedness, crime, brutality, murder, and wars? If people are basically good by nature, why are there so many lawyers and lawsuits? Why a need for police and prisons? If everyone is basically good at heart, why are so many people chronically offended, enraged, and violent? Why can't eight billion good people just get along, right? Apparently, the simplicity of the golden rule, "Do to others as you would have them do to you," is not so easy to live by.

The sobering truth of the matter that "enlightened" modern man keeps trying to brush aside is this: We are not as good as we like to think, and more capable of worse than we want to admit. Put simply, we are sinful. We sin against each other, in thoughts, words and deeds.

But how often do you hear anyone in private or public life ask for forgiveness? Come right out and use that word? Instead, there's a constant parade of excuses and blame shifting. "I misspoke." "You took me out of context." "I didn't mean it that way." "You took it wrong." And the classic, "I'm sorry that offended you."

When someone does make an apology, it sounds scripted by a PR department and includes a carefully worded plausible explanation. It's simply for show, a deflection or smoke screen. But even apologies are risky. They can trigger lawsuits. Nobody wants to own up to nuthin'. Certainly not sin.

Sin has been downgraded to mistakes, missteps, and poor choices. In fact, sin has not just been downgraded, there is an attempt to scrub it from the English language. I bet hardly anyone knows that in 2014, the Oxford English Dictionary removed the word "sin." Why? According to the illuminated overseers of the famous dictionary, quote, "it has fallen into disuse and is not recognized by the younger generation." Sounds Orwellian, right? Change reality by changing language. Apparently, there are Shinola hucksters even at Oxford. There's an old Southern saying that goes: You can call a pile of cow manure ice cream, but it still tastes like crap.

So, why all this wordplay? Calling sin merely a mistake, misstep or error implies that what we did or said was unintentional or merely an oversight. Just a slip of the tongue, not a fracture in the soul. It was "uncharacteristic" of us, not a core character flaw. Can you see the motive? Lessen the severity of our actions and avoid responsibility for them. "I'm OK. You're OK. No harm, no foul. We good?"

The deflection dance starts young. "He hit me first!" "I didn't mean to knock her down." "It was an accident." A 70s comedian, Flip Wilson, created a character named Geraldine whose constant excuse for her behavior was, "The devil made me do it!" Blame-shifting abounds.

The reality is this. We haven't come very far from the fig leaf cover-up episode in the Garden of Eden. All the verbal shifting, rationalizing and PR airbrushing are just attempts to cover our guilt and shame. And without guilt and shame, who needs to ask forgiveness? More crucial to the broken state of the world, who needs saving from being basically good? (See the letter: Savior vs. Hero)

You all once went through a phase of asking me stories about my life. "Tell us a lifetime," you would say. Well, here's one I'm not very proud of.

I once told a "little" lie at the vehicle registration office. I was out of town quite a lot back then and my license plate had expired. By a couple of months. The clerk said if I hadn't driven the car in that time period, I could save a few dollars by changing the registration date. She pushed a piece of paper across the counter for me to sign. I read these ominous words: "Under penalty of perjury I confirm this vehicle has not been driven" between such-and-such dates. I signed it. Paid a few dollars less and went to my car. Had I ever lied before? Ok, maybe a few times. Had I ever signed my name to a lie? Never. It got to me. I went back inside to the same clerk and told her I made a "mistake." That I needed to redo the registration. She looked at me, grinned, smacked her gum and said, "You lied, didn't you?" She turned around to the rest of the office and, in a voice plenty loud enough for everyone to hear, announced, "Hey, we got an honest man here. He lied on his form and can't live with it." I endured their laughter, redid the form, paid the full amount and got out as quick as I could. I felt pretty good about my triumph of conscience until it hit me: I was willing to sell my integrity for about twenty-five bucks.

Was my little lie a mistake? Nope. It was a sin. What's the commandment? Thou shalt not knowingly misrepresent facts or motives with the intent to deceive, except in small circumstances for profit, appearances or political gain? Nope. It just says, "Thou shalt not lie."

The other side of forgiveness is forgiving someone who has hurt us. "Trespassed against us" as the Lord's prayer puts it. I'm not sure which is harder, asking for forgiveness or giving it. Both require humility and courage.

In some situations, I took way too long to learn the benefit and beauty of forgiving someone. It's a hard lesson. Forgiving a wound from someone that keeps hurting us seems unreasonable and counterintuitive. We tell ourselves, if the offender would just ask for forgiveness, it would hurt less. That would satisfy our need for justice, too. And that can certainly bring some healing. But why is it, even if the offender owns their crappy behavior, the wound keeps hurting?

Here's the key, the part you should highlight, so I'll set it apart.

> Forgiving makes healing in us possible,
> whether the offender asks for it or not.

This, my beloved brood, will set you free. It's how forgiving becomes divine. Because it's like the forgiveness God gives us. Jesus said, "Forgive one another *as I have forgiven you.*" His forgiveness was divine. Ours can be, too.

> To forgive is to set a prisoner free
> and to discover the prisoner was you.
>
> Corrie Ten Boom

Well, one more "lifetime" and I'll wrap this up.

I already told you about my haircut incident with my dad my freshman year of college. (See the letter: Significance vs. Success) But here's a recap and a little more detail about how it played out.

I arrived home from college on a Wednesday at Thanksgiving my freshman year. A quirky friend with very long hair came with me. My hair had grown quite a bit, but no longer than the early Beatles' moptops. Everyone but Dad greeted me warmly at the kitchen door. As I set my stuff down in the living room, he walked in. His first words to me were, "Damn, look at your hair." He was not pleased.

Early next morning, he woke me up to get a haircut from a barber who agreed to open his shop. On Thanksgiving Day! My friend went with us. We drove in silence. Got my haircut. Drove back in silence. I was mortified.

Fast forward about thirty years. On a visit to my parents, we were looking at a photo album from that time. Dad recalled the Thanksgiving haircut incident. I hadn't thought of it in many years. He looked at me and very humbly said, "Bill, I shouldn't have done that. I'm really sorry. I hope you can forgive me." It was obvious he really regretted it. I had forgiven him long before he asked for it. What a divine moment. We actually had a good laugh remembering another Christmas when I came home with a beard he didn't know about. He already had an electric razor under the tree for me! I chuckle now remembering all that. And miss him.

I guess it won't surprise you if I use a hit song from 1989 to sum all this up.

I've been trying to get down to the heart of the matter...
I think it's about forgiveness, forgiveness
Even if, even if, you don't love me anymore
The Heart of the Matter by Don Henley
from "The End of the Innocence"

You sure got it right, Don.

My hallowed humans, we are saints and sinners. We are of immeasurable worth, made in the image of God. But we are broken, not by our mistakes. By sin. Thank God, as Alistair Begg, one of my favorite preachers, puts it, once we are saved, "sin doesn't reign, but it remains." And so, this side of heaven, we will likely never outgrow our need to ask forgiveness and forgive those who trespass against us.

With the wounds you get and the wounds you give, I hope you can get down to the heart of the matter quicker than I did. Ask for forgiveness. And give it. In order to experience the beauty and freedom of that healing spiritual reality.

Thank God, we're not on our own in this. We have help to know when we've blown it.

Search me, God, and know my heart;
Test me and know my anxious thoughts.
See if there is any offensive way in me,
and lead me in the way everlasting.
Psalm 139:23,24

Only two more things to say. My dear children, please, forgive me for any clueless, careless or callous ways I've wounded you. Wyatt, thank you for forgiving me that day in the car. When I'm too old and feeble to fasten my seatbelt, you may get to help me, but very likely with more compassion.

Love, Dad

Letter 21

True Love vs. *Infatuation*

When I wake from dreaming, tell me
Is it really love? How will I know?

Whitney Houston

My undeserved treasures,

This is a tough letter to write. My track record in this area might seem to disqualify me from giving you input about this. But even those of us who have loved and lost know what we lost. What we miss. And still long for. Namely, a forever love, tender, true, and all in, come what may. That's what I hope for you. In fact, since you were toddlers, I've prayed you will each find true love.

I've written to you already how beauty can be an unreliable gauge by which to measure a person. (See the letter: Virtue vs. Beauty) Unfortunately, our culture values beauty (and talent) far above character. My generation wasn't any different. Historically, beauty has always been seductive. When we are young (or immature at any age), external beauty and sex appeal are hypnotic lures. Of course, physical attraction is part of the dance, but marketing and hormones make it very difficult to see beyond the externals.

For instance, I dated a gorgeous girl in college, dark hair, mysterious, voluptuous, who turned out to be a sad, hollow soul.

Full disclosure, my soul and faith were not rock solid then either. Between her looks and my hormones, I was like a fly in a spider web. Men, boys rather, had pursued her for her beauty. So did I. By the time we got around to going below the surface, it was clear our relationship wasn't built on much. Her empty plus my flimsy did not make for true love.

After college, a beautiful, talented young woman told me she heard God say I was going to be her husband. I was deeply in love with her and admired her as a person. We shared much in common. A life together seemed just ahead. Only months later, she changed her mind. I was devastated. Apparently, I was in love, but she was either just infatuated or misread the memo from God. True love takes two.

So, Whitney Houston's song, *How Will I Know*, is spot-on. How do you know when it's truly love or a Shinola dream?

There's a saying, "when you know you know." But that is really no help at all. And what if your "knower" gets broken from a few failed relationships that "felt" like love but didn't work out?

Well, there's your first red flag: feelings. Feelings are great. There is no high like being in love. As Whitney sang, "I lose control, can't seem to get enough... I fall in love whenever we meet." But like beauty, feelings can be intoxicating. Who doesn't enjoy walking on air? Head in the clouds. But, news flash: feelings are less than a reliable indicator of a lasting love. In fact, for some, falling in love is like an addiction. Hordes are in love with being in love. But when the feelings subside, feet touch back down on the ground, gullible hearts tend to believe only a new romance will relight the fire. I guess it wouldn't surprise you I co-wrote a song about that.

She fell in love with love songs and fairy tales
She runs away from the first sign her fantasy could fail
Everything she knows about love
Is just make believe from silver screens
It'll never be enough
She is in love with love songs and fairy tales

But true love is not a spell,
A perfect rhyme, no wishing well
In true love there's no pretending
It's not a moment, it's never-ending

Love Songs and Fairy Tales
by Cam Monroe, Joe Beck & me

The addictive quality of romantic love is not a new thing. In Shakespeare's time, Francis Bacon, the British philosopher and scientist, said this about the euphoria of being in love: "It is impossible to love and be wise." Yes, I co-wrote a song with that, too. (though never been recorded) Here's a verse and chorus.

I think I'll take my chances
Better to love and lose
Than never know the feeling
Of walking on air, pleasantly confused

Call me a double fool for loving and not hiding
I lose my common sense deep in your eyes

147

I know I'm rushing in, But what's the use in fighting
There's no way to love and be wise

To Love and Be Wise
by Wayne Kirkpatrick and me

We are all prone to rush in because we're hungry (more like famished) to love and be loved. It's how we're wired. We were made to love and be loved. (Wrote that song, too. But will spare you that one.) It's not surprising we often go to extremes to satisfy that hunger. You've seen it. A great woman dates a rascal (spelled j-a-c-k-a-s-s) of a guy. No one can understand why she puts with him. She could do much better. And the reverse happens, too. A fairly solid man endures emotional abuse from a toxic, self-centered, shall we say, undercooked soul of a girlfriend?

My truelove hunters, what if I told you there is a way to love and be wise? A way to walk into love, eyes open, instead of "falling" in love, which sounds like having an accident. There is another, better way to find true love. Not a foolproof way, because humans can be elaborately layered and camouflaged in the persona we each present to the world. But these few things will move the odds in your favor of not being mesmerized and deceived by beauty and charm. (See the letter: Character vs. Charisma)

Again, full disclosure: I've learned these things by failing to apply them in some relationships. But have also enjoyed the power and benefit of them.

First, long before your interest even lands on someone, decide what kind of someone you want to land with. In fact, make a list. A lot of the titles to these letters contain attributes in couples who've found forever love: faithful, admirable, kind, good character, courageous, joyful, wise, forgiving, selfless. Sounds like a tall order, huh? Most forever couples add another ingredient: humor. They make each other laugh.

You can find some of these qualities and more in 1 Corinthians 13, which is read at many weddings. It describes what love, ergo, a loving person is like. It's probably worth including here:

Love is *patient*.
Love is *kind*.
It does *not envy* (i.e., is secure).
It does *not boast*.
It is *not proud* (i.e., is humble).
It does *not dishonor* others.
It is not *self-seeking*. (See the letter: Usie vs. Selfie)
It is *not easily angered* (i.e., is self-controlled).
It keeps *no record of wrongs* (i.e., forgives and lets stuff go).
Love does *not delight in evil, but rejoices in the truth*.
Love always *protects*, always *trusts*, always hopes, always *perseveres*.

Finding someone like that would go beyond wow to awe. (See the letter: Awe vs. Wow) Here's an all-caps clue to finding someone like that. BE SOMEONE LIKE THAT. I'm glad to say I can see you are on your way there.

Once you set your viewfinder on these things, there is far less chance you will fall for someone who is merely a hunk or babe, but berates people (and you) when they are not around, is hollow on the inside, lets dishes, laundry, bills and issues stack up, drinks or spends in secret, or drowns stray cats in their spare time.

I'm not saying you can't be over the moon about someone. Read *Song of Songs*. It's steamy. That couple was beyond gone on each other, body and soul.

Second, once your heart and mind (both, not either) set sight on a "could be the one" who has many of these qualities, you will begin to know why you know. Hopefully, this will lead you to begin not with "I love you because I can't stop thinking about you and your smile, your kiss, or keep my hands off you." But with this: "I love who you are." This comes from seeing below the surface. That's when you will know the relationship has truelove possibilities.

Third, the time factor. Does truelove happen at first sight? Yes, but the cases of that are a blessed, not lucky, minority. (See the letter: Blessed vs. Lucky) Seeing each other in the challenges and flow of daily life, under stress, with family and friends, in work dynamics, is a revealing discovery zone. It takes time to really see and know a person. I already quoted this famous playwright in the letter, Dignity vs. Ego, but it bears repeating here.

Nobody sees anybody truly, but all through the flaws of
their own egos... except when there is that rare case of
two people who love intensely enough to burn through all
those layers of opacity and see each other's naked hearts.
Tennessee Williams - playwright

"Opacity" Good word. It means "lacking transparency." Add opacity's opposite to the list of truelove's qualities: transparent.

Since Tennessee Williams brought it up, let's talk about "naked." I was going to write you a letter titled "Intimacy vs. Eros" (Eros being sexual passion), but it fits to address that here, too.

You already know some of my regrettable history and failures in this area. As I said in the opening letter, my hope is that you will be less scarred and more blessed than me.

When Tennessee Williams says "naked hearts" that doesn't mean the physical closeness of sex. There can be physical passion without intimacy. "Naked hearts" means intimacy, a nearness, a communing of heart, soul and mind. Not a body thing.

The pattern of this world, and certainly our sex-obsessed culture, is to experience naked bodies before naked hearts. And equate physical passion with love. This behavior is understandable for those whose worldview is: Eat, drink, be merry, pursue as much pleasure as you can, because there's nothing but lights out at the end of the road. (See the letter: Heaven vs. Sky)

I guess I don't have to point out that the pattern of this world rarely jives with God's way of doing things. By sheer physiology, it's easy to think that the way he hot-wired us for physical passion sets us up for failure. Especially in the face of his more difficult self-denying way to bless us - monogamy and the sacred intimacy of the marriage bed. Who can color within those lines when it seems almost everyone is coloring outside them, or erasing the lines altogether? Holding back such a natural drive is not easy. Does this verse sound like God doesn't get that? "But if they cannot control themselves, they should marry, for it is better to marry than to burn with passion." (1 Corinthians 7:9) Read that entire section, verses 1 to 9. God gets it. He's the one who gave us burning passions!

By saving sex for marriage, some think God is intent on keeping us from having fun. Not so. His better way includes all this:

So go and eat your food now and enjoy it. Drink your wine and be happy. It is all right with God if you do these things. Wear nice clothes and make yourself look good. Enjoy life with the wife [or husband] you love.

Ecclesiastes 9:7-9

Most people don't know that's in the Bible. Even more spicy and detailed, just read Song of Songs. God is all in on the joy of romance and sex.

In fact, from the beginning, before the fig leaf incident, Adam and Eve were "naked and unashamed." Imagine that. How freeing would that be? If you aim for that, and walk out that vision, you will experience a blessing the masses miss out on by buying into the Shinola of "love the one you're with" and "let's get it on." You know I failed in that area. I missed out on the beauty of that blessing. But God can give us a reset. Your mother and I waited until our wedding night to be "naked and unashamed." Whatever else we messed up, we got that part right.

Thank God, we can mess up, and receive forgiveness and pardon. God is beyond generous with grace. He certainly has been for me. We can struggle and fail and begin again. But the pattern of our culture is simply to flip the script to "don't fight the feeling" and view sex as just a step in getting to know someone.

Let's play that game we used to play on the way to school – One of these things is not like the other. Spot what is *not* Shinola.

a) You can have everything marriage offers, without marriage.
b) Sex is a natural expression of love and will bring you closer together.
c) If you can't be with the one you love, honey, love the one you're with. (CS&N 1970)
d) Truelove is a just a fairy tale.
e) No one buys a car without a test drive.
f) At the beginning the Creator made them male and female and said 'For this reason a man will leave his father and mother and be united to his wife, and the two will become one flesh. (Matthew 19:4,5. Jesus quoting Genesis 2:24)
g) No one buys a dairy cow before tasting the milk.

OK, I made that pretty obvious. These brands of Shinola have been selling for a long time. My generation claims to have started the "sexual revolution." But the Roman culture made the 1960s look tame. In love and romance, Sacred has clearly taken a back seat to Shinola for a long, long time.

My high-aiming hearts, as always, two roads diverge into the world. I pray you choose more wisely and sooner in this area that I did. And take the road God assures will lead to your good and best, and good and best for your spouse and children. By waiting, you will build trust, honor and affirm the value of your mate, and strengthen the sanctity of your marriage.

Besides experiencing the fullness of one of God's best gifts, there are other reasons to wait to give yourself physically to your forever love in marriage. You will avoid some heartaches and possible tangles, like a nasty STD or an oops pregnancy, with all its complexity and mixed blessings.

And while we're being real, let's face it. Even for the strong in faith, a list of reasons and benefits can disappear like warm Krispy Kreme donuts in the heat of the moment.

Should you choose the donuts, or wait for the feast, God is good and merciful enough to provide restoration and a way back to blessing. Though not without some loss and consequences. For instance, the anxious and humbling conversation to tell your truelove you have not been true or pure; and the mental battle of having sexual memories with others that don't easily erase, and which can resurface to complicate being naked and unashamed with your truelove. But again, there is healing and restoration in the Lord's merciful ways. "Love covers a multitude of sins." (1 Peter 4:8) I'm sure my "hallelujah" is not the only one about that.

Choosing the sacred path has never been easy. The reason "true and pure" sound so old fashioned these days is a measure of how much Shinola has taken hearts and minds captive. But the grandeur of the prize for those who choose it, or who may fail and rechoose it, outshines anything Shinola can offer.

Someday, I hope to celebrate with each of you and your truelove at your weddings. I'm sure you will pick a special song for your first dance. Maybe it will speak things like this.

Forever Love

Everybody wants a love that lasts forever
That's what I was lookin' for when I found you

I knew the day you took my hand we'd be together
And I could go the distance with a love so strong
So tender and true

I'm gonna love you
Rain or Shine - Day and Night,
Till the last star tumbles from the sky
I will be by your side, till the day I die
I'm gonna hold you
Til the Oceans dry up
Til the tallest Mountain turns to dust
One Lifetime's not enough, to be lovin' you because
This is Forever Love - you're my Forever Love

Forever Love by Joe Beck and me

I will probably cry and toast to a long and happy lifetime for you and your forever love. Here's to that joyful day.

Love, Dad

Letter 22

Heaven vs. *Sky*

Imagine there's no heaven, It's easy if you try,
No hell below us, above us only sky.

John Lennon - from "Imagine"

My earth angels,

Let me make a prediction. You will likely never attend a
Christian funeral where someone sings the song, *Imagine*. Imagine
though, that somewhere in this crazy world a group of imaginers
gathers at the memorial for a friend. Someone stands and offers
that song as a declaration of sheer courage against the finality of
death and the nothingness beyond this life - which the famous
song expresses. Picture the hollowness of that event.

Imagine the main speaker stands and says, "Our friend was
here. Now our friend is nothing but a memory. And once we are
all dead, he will not even be that. And we're all headed for the
same fate. Have a nice day."

Then a pianist plays the familiar opening to the song. A singer
begins. Let me offer a more direct translation of *Imagine* on one
level as the song rolls out over the crowd attempting, but failing,
to soften the despair:

Imagine there's no meaning
In all we do or say
No one and nothing matters
We're just matter anyway
Imagine all the people
As one big worm buffet

You–hoo-oo-oo-oo, you may say I'm a downer,
But I'm not the only one
I hope you know hope is hopeless
In the meantime, lunch is on

The last chord rings into silence. Someone near the back breaks the awkwardness with a feeble, "Right on." Then everyone, family first, shuffles out to the reception to tell stories about the deceased over finger sandwiches and bunt cake.

Imagine. John Lennon, clearly one of the most inventive songwriters and musicians of all time, not imagining anything beyond what he can see – not considering the possibility of a realm beyond this world - or conceiving a power above and beyond his own mind. How could such a creative imagination not picture anything more beautiful or lasting than a completely earthbound version of a thing called "love".

John sang, "You may say I'm a dreamer." Maybe he wasn't such a big dreamer after all. It seems sad that such an imaginative songwriter could write a truly beautiful piece of music like that for the purpose of unifying the planet, but point people, perhaps unintentionally, toward despair.

But hang on, you know how much I love the music of the Beatles. For me, *The Long and Winding Road* is not just one of the deepest, saddest love songs ever written. On another level, it's one of the deepest spiritual journey songs, too. As Paul said about it, "The road leads not to Campbeltown, but to somewhere you never expected." Maybe there is more than meets the ear in John's song, too, that accounts for its global appeal. I'll get back to that.

* * *

I heard a story of another songwriter who had a dream. One night, he dreamed he died and went to heaven. An angelic being met him and escorted him through the pearly gates. As they entered glory, the songwriter heard music begin in the distance. It grew louder. And seemed very familiar. After a moment, the identity of the song hit him. Turning to his heavenly companion, he blurted out with great amazement, "They're singing one of my songs!"

The angel smiled, leaned close to the songwriter and said with the joy of revealing a long-kept secret, "No, you've been singing one of ours."

* * *

My big dreamers, one of the centerpiece questions of all time, is this: "Is there life beyond this life?" It has been asked in every generation, by every curious, mortal heart. Is there more to life than meets the eye? Are we actually spirits walking around in meat suits? Is there more than sky above us? Are we more than the dust to which our bodies return? John's haunting song seems to answer these questions – no. What we see is all we get.

To give him the benefit of the doubt, maybe John's intent was rhetorical, for the sake of bettering our situation on the planet. IF there's nothing beyond this life, how do we best get along with each other? He certainly seemed to be all about peace and love.

Like millions of people, I was heartbroken when John Lennon was murdered. Suddenly gone. But gone where?

This kind of question arises out of a deep longing. One very wise man wrote about the source of it:

"God has placed eternity in man's heart, yet so that he cannot understand what God has done from beginning to end."

(Ecclesiastes 3:11)

So, while we don't have all the answers to scratch every itch, we do have the itch, the deep longing, awareness, and hope for eternity - for something beyond the sky. And that itch is our compass heading, too. It points us beyond the sky, beyond the last beat of our heart. It points to wonder. To the wonder of creation. And of God. Eternity. And who we are - here and beyond here.

Most people on our planet still lean toward this hope. It makes my heart glad that you do, too.

However, more and more people are turning from this hope to atheism and a worldview called existentialism, that we exist only in a physical world. It's a view that says, "what we see is all we get." Some even claim that this longing, this soul itch, leads to religion, which they consider a primary cause of the ills in the world. This growing number of Shinola shouters like to rant and rave that religion keeps people from really waking up to our true situation - that we are merely very organized, evolved animals who over a long process of trial and error have created language and airplanes, chia pets and computers, guitars and art, ice cream and the internet. Their solution is that by throwing off this nagging eternal itch, we can all come together for the common good around beautiful, sad songs, and free finger sandwiches and bunt cake for everyone.

For a lot of people, the sky really is the limit. *Imagine* has become their anthem, their rally cry. It's still among the biggest hits one of the Beatles ever had.

On one level, John's elegant song imagines that our deepest longing is wrong. But ask this. Has the worldview the song advocates worked at all to rid the world of religion, of countries and borders, of causes to live or die for, of greed or hunger, of current wars, or the next one? Has it moved us closer to a world where all people are just "living for today," in brotherhood and in peace? Has John's vision and those who believe in it awakened the masses deceived by religion and led them out of darkness into a balanced, enlightened unity of shared loneliness in a Godless universe? Has the song even made a scratch on the itch? Not so much.

In fact, on another level, I think John's haunting music speaks louder than the lyric, and in the opposite direction. The lovely melody makes the itch for eternity even more persistent. It does mine. His words describe a place of universal peace and harmony, on earth, but only tips a hat to the invisible elephant in the poetry. Death. Our mortality. He wrote, "Nothing to kill or die for." But doesn't even hint of a hope beyond that. Beyond a shared world free of need and greed. That's why it's an unlikely funeral song. Hopeless doesn't go down well in that setting.

My eternal flesh and blood blessings, I have more than a hunch that the powerful thing the music of *Imagine* taps into is a universal longing below and counter to the lyric. As much as John might have wanted to imagine a world freed of "flawed" religious thinking, he could not escape the itch himself. In fact, something he once said about God revealed a reality that scripture itself affirms. Lennon said,

"I believe in God, but not as one thing, not as an old man. In the sky. I believe that what people call God is, something in all of us."

Imagine John getting so close to this truth about a divine spark and not seeing the bigger picture. But that's exactly what scripture says.

He [God] has set eternity in the human heart; yet no one can fathom what God has done from beginning to end.

Ecclesiastes 3:11

John Lennon, the rock icon, the talented lad from Liverpool, actually had the itch, the divine spark. Like all of us, he couldn't fathom the immensity of God and the panorama of the Creator's creative genius and plan. Maybe, like all of us, he was blinded by ego. (See the letter Dignity vs. Ego) Add worldwide fame and crazy wealth to that and any of us might design and declare our own opinion of the cosmos.

Clearly, John longed for something like heaven. But a heaven here on earth. Next time you listen to it, see if you don't hear the melancholy beauty of the music dripping with the eternity God set in John's heart? I hear it. Could it be that longing is what connects so many people with his song? Even those trying so hard to scratch the eternal itch with philosophy, pleasure, political power, success, causes and poetry?

Who can say whether in his final years or moments John Lennon actually hoped for something beyond this life or cried out to God as his life here flickered away in seconds on his last evening? December 8, 1980. I hope and pray so. His last words were, "I'm shot!" He knew what was happening.

I can imagine the Lord receiving John's soul in that transition from lying on a New York City sidewalk into glory. I can imagine the Lord smiling at him with all his grace and goodness, saying, "Surprised? Walk with me, John." As they head off into the soul-captivating panorama beyond even a Beatles' imagination, the Lord, as a lighthearted touch between the two of them, hums the melody to *Imagine*. The wry humor is not lost on John. Then, from every direction, the heavenly host of angels and saints begin to sing *All You Need Is Love*. Imagine John realizing, with wonder and humility that on earth he had been singing one of heaven's songs that leaked into his creative process, and became a big hit for the Fab 4. I can imagine there amid that indescribable glory, John awakens and marvels at a place where there is no need to be a dreamer. The dream has come. The itch is gone. The dreamer is home. Meanwhile, over his shoulder on this side of heaven, the invitation of his classic song takes on new meaning for him. "I hope someday you'll join us."

One starry, early summer night, when fireflies were still out, we set up our camping tent in the backyard by the fire pit. Sawyer, you weren't on the planet yet. Willow and Wyatt, you were about five and four. We were planning to spend the whole night, but when you fell asleep we carried you to bed to escape the mosquitos. I sat up late by the fire and wrote a song with you in mind about the itch. Maybe all my songs are about the itch in one way or another.

> Fireflies hold back the dying day
> It's a valiant effort
> Stars start to dance up in the haze
> And the shy moon is on the run
> Through the night till morning comes
> Dressed in silken flames of glory
>
> This life is a canvas on fire, burn bright
> Live your deepest desire for the time
> Here on this side of heaven will fly
> Like sparks in the night
> This life is a gift from the One
> Who gives life,
> To every daughter and son take the time
> Here on this side of heaven to find
> The road that goes on and on... on beyond this life

> *This Life* from Soundtrack of My Soul

My dear dreamers, learn to live with the itch. In fact, be grateful for it. Let it move you to wonder and awe, remind you who you are and assure you the journey we are on leads beyond this life. Let it comfort you, not as an eventual escape from this world, but as an intimate touch from the One who placed the itch there. And let the itch move you to be of great earthly good to the spirits in meat suits all around who are itching for heaven, too, but often feeling a little lost, lonely and insignificant under an ever-changing sky.

Jesus actually described this itch as a thirst. He said only a certain kind of "living" water could quench it. A water that doesn't rain from the sky, but flows from a higher place - a place I can only imagine. That sounds like another song I love. It's sung at a lot of memorial services.

Surrounded by your glory what will my heart feel?
Will I dance for you, Jesus, or in awe of you be still?
Will I stand in your presence or to my knees will I fall?
Will I sing "Halleluia" will I be able to speak at all?
I can only imagine… I can only imagine."

I Can Only Imagine by Bart Millard

So far, I've only met one Beatle, Ringo, briefly after his concert in Nashville. When he shook my hand, all I could think to say was, "Thank you for all the music." He simply said in his Liverpool accent, "Ooh, you're welcome." I hope when I get to heaven, I get to meet two other Beatles. Ultimately, all of them. At the end of this long and winding road. And thank them for the music. Imagine that.

Love, Dad

Letter 23

God vs. *Gold*

Money won't make you happy,
but everyone wants to find out for themselves.

Zig Ziglar – author

My golden gang,

I'm grateful you are all hard workers, even enterprising. You already have a better perspective on money, its value and purpose than I had at your age. I was mostly growing my hair and guitar skills.

Willow, you started your first company when you were eleven - Willow's Wonder Works. You even had a business card! After your Great Aunt Annie taught you how to crochet, you dove in to making things: warm caps for babies, heating bags filled with seeds and rice to help with sore muscles, and flip-flops with colorfully wrapped foot straps. You sold them at your booth at craft festivals. From those early earnings, you practiced giving and saving. And still do.

Wyatt, the day you got your first bike, you spent two hours riding it up and down the driveway until you mastered it. You applied the same focus to selling golf balls we retrieved from a pond on hole number three behind our house. Day after day one summer, you and Willow loaded up camping chairs, an umbrella, drinks and snacks and a wagonload of sorted golf balls to sell beside the tee box on the eighth hole. Before summer was over, we walked into a computer store where you bought your first Mac laptop - with cash. And had money left over. That same focus and determination made you a great drummer from your start on a set of toy drums from Toys "R" US. I wouldn't trade all those noisy hours you practiced in your room for all the peace and quiet in the world. You don't know this, but I recorded bits of your practice sessions on my phone outside your door just so I can always have a sample of the rhythm of you.

Sawyer, after many years of playing soccer like your brother, when you took up tennis you dove all in. You made the school team and in a few months beat opponents who had been playing for many years. Your landscape boss told me, "Congratulations. You've raised a hard worker." That's music to a dad's ears. (Of course, that's in contrast to how long you could wait to unload the dishwasher or clean your bathroom;) With the example and help of your sister and brother, you already have a Roth IRA set up and make small, steady investments from what you earn at multiple jobs.

Bravo! You all have investment and savings accounts. You have short and long views of money. The hourly wage and tip jobs you've done have given you a sense of the value of things. Like, how many work hours do you have to trade for a concert ticket, a new snare head, or tennis racket?

A wise friend asked me a question that gets to the heart of the matter. "What's your relationship with money?" Think about that. Edmund Burke, an Irish economist and philosopher said this:

Money is a good servant but a bad master.

Which is it for you? A servant or master? There are ways of telling. How does a bump up in money affect your spending? Giving? And saving? How does a shortage affect all those? Does your emotional peace rise and fall with your bank accounts or the stock market? Is what you earn all "my" money?

Remember the Christmas of the money miracle? I described that in the letter Kind vs. Nice. No need to retell the details here, except to say out of the blue, just over $13K showed up at our house one morning from friends. More than $10K of it anonymous!

We witnessed the goodness of the Lord from the hands of those for whom money was a servant. Remember how stunned and blessed we were? Imagine the joy of the ones who blessed us. (See the letter: Joy vs. Happiness) Besides blowing my mind and heart, that will always be a powerful example of money as a good servant.

So, we work, right? And God provides. Beyond what we can imagine. But is all we earn or are given our own? Like the Parable of the Talents illustrates (Matthew 15), we are entrusted with time, talent and treasure for purposes beyond us and our needs. (See the letter: Significance vs. Success)

God knows our hearts and hands tend to hold too tight to money. That it can woo us away from his best and highest for us. So, he reminded his people early on.

You may say to yourself, "My power and the strength of my hands have produced this wealth for me." But remember the Lord your God, forit is he who gives you the ability to produce wealth. Deuteronomy 8:17

As in most things, when it comes to money, this world turns things upside down. It trades what's sacred for shiny things. The new golden rule seems to be, "Whoever rules the gold makes the rules." But as a more famous William wrote, "All that glitters is not gold." *(Shakespeare from The Merchant of Venice)* Our Christmas miracle made that clear. Kindness and generosity shine brighter.

Jesus made it plain.

Do not store up for yourselves treasures on earth…
but store up for yourselves treasures in heaven…
for where your treasure is, there your heart will be also.

Jesus - Matthew 6:21

Those who helped us that Christmas stored up great treasure in heaven. We can, too.

So, my talented troupe, give, save, invest, spend. Even in tight financial times, keep giving, even a little, to something you care about. Like supporting veterans through Tunnel 2 Towers or Wounded Warrior Project. Samaritan's purse for disaster relief. Or sponsor a child monthly through Compassion International or World Vision. There is always a need we can help meet if money is our servant. Not our master.

Knowing the source of your time, talent and treasure, be generous with them all. Why settle for the Shinola of the uncertainty of wealth? Instead, work hard and trust in God, who richly provides. He blesses so we can bless others. But remember, our ultimate ROI (return on investment) is eternal. (1st Timothy 6:17-19)

I thank God for entrusting you to me. You're my priceless legacy. I know you don't always feel shiny, but your souls are living proof that all that glitters is not gold.

Love, Dad

Letter 24

Identity vs. *Title*

Part of me suspects that I'm a loser,
and the other part of me thinks I'm God Almighty.
John Lennon - Beatle

My treasures in jars of clay,

Sawyer, once upon a time when you were six or seven, we were playing ping pong. It was the first time I noticed you could hit the ball back and forth four or five times in a row. At one point, I said, "Man, you're really getting better at this!"

You blurted out, "Yea, and I haven't even practiced. It's just God in me."

Talk about "out of the mouths of babes." Good one, son. Bullseye. I bet you didn't know that expression, "out of the mouths of babes," comes from the Bible, Psalm 8:2. Your witty remark is at the heart of what I want to say in this letter.

A question kids get asked a lot is: What do you want to be when you grow up? The answers are usually job descriptions, like some of your answers: a professional soccer player, a singer, an entrepreneur, an engineer, video editor, a drummer. One of my early answers was marine biologist, just because I always loved whales. The heart of a blue whale is as big as a VW Bug! A full grown person can crawl through it! Awe-mazing, huh.

The typical answers to that question, about what to be as a grownup, point to what title you wear in your job as an adult.

We all have titles. A title answers the question: What do you do for a living? There's no shortage of them. Sales associate, VP of Marketing, teacher, standup comedian, real estate agent, cetologist (someone who studies whales). Some titles describe a phase of life. Toddler, Teenager, Gen Z, Gen X, Middle-aged, Baby boomer. Some labels refer to our view on things or groups we belong to. Democrat, Republican, Independent, Libertarian, Baptist, Catholic, Pentecostal, atheist, Sigma Chi, Eagle Scout. The lists go on and on.

My own titles include: Dad (one of my favorites), Christian, songwriter, author, baby boomer, hair-challenged (not my favorite).

Titles are useful. But if we only have a title to define us by what we do, rather than who we are, they can become Shinola, an external veneer to present to the world and define our function in it. A title can't tell the whole story.

Identity begs a different question than what do you do? Identity poses one of the most crucial questions in this life:

Who am I?

Behind the titles and labels. Underneath. At our core. Who are we? The answer to that makes all the difference in the world.

My observant offspring, you may have noticed there's a lot of confusion out there about identity. Ask ten people, "Who are you? Not what do you do for a living?" and you'll likely get ten different answers. From King of Kool to a lover of whales. But at our core nature, who are we?

America's founders answered that question by affirming an a priori assumption (a foundational building block) that our core nature is this: we are created by a Creator who gives us basic, self-evident rights. (See the letters: Joy vs. Happiness and Dignity vs. Ego) That implies a whale of a lot of things I can't get into here. (See what I did there?)

In the time since that famous declaration, an incremental yet growing current of thought has eroded that building block about who we are. Many people prefer a more "enlightened" view that we are basically dust in the winds of time and chance, highly evolved animals, to be congratulated on our rise to prominence on the planet. That we are nothing more than the king of the beasts. We live. We roar. We go whimpering back to dust. Case closed. This view has had catastrophic effects on human behavior and societies at large. Again, too much to serve up here. This sums it up well.

The present American society is stuck because it views humanity as a cosmic chemical accident, existing with no intentional origin, with no noble destiny and so with no path through history.

George Weigel
from his intro to *Light of the World*

The two worldviews could not be more opposed. Are we created by God? Or a random product of time, space, chance and unconscious matter, forced into a purposeless struggle for survival in a meaningless cycle of suffering and intermittent pleasure? Are our souls destined for a purposeful life and glorious eternity or doomed to the treadmill of a job title and beyond that the grave and oblivion?

Sawyer, your witty response, "It's just God in me" hits the heart, the epicenter of meaning, purpose, and above all, our identity. If God is not at the heart of us and the universe, we are truly lost in the cosmos bearing only tags like: Assistant Regional Manager, CEO, Exterminator or Golf Pro. And at the end, a toe tag in the morgue. In that case, we are certainly, as John Lennon sensed, losers. Big losers.

It also seems abundantly clear, based on our obvious limitations, one thing we are not is God Almighty. And not in charge. Job got an eloquent reminder of this from God himself.

Where were you when I laid the earth's foundation?
Tell me, if you understand.
Who marked off its dimensions? Surely you know!
Who stretched a measuring line across it?
On what were its footings set,
or who laid its cornerstone—
while the morning stars sang together
and all the angels shouted for joy?
Who shut up the sea behind doors
when it burst forth from the womb,
when I made the clouds its garment
and wrapped it in thick darkness,
when I fixed limits for it

and set its doors and bars in place,

when I said, 'This far you may come and no farther;

here is where your proud waves halt'?

Job 38:4-11

God goes on for three more chapters about His resume, describing what only He can do because of who he is. Read it for yourself. Is there anyone on the planet evolved enough to pull off any of that? I'll wait...

Job's answer was silence and repentance.

I put my hand over my mouth... I will say no more. Job 40:3,4
...and repent in dust and ashes. Job 42:6

Wise move, Job. God is God. And we are not.

My nimble spirits in a material world, what if in one sense we are dust? That matches the Genesis account.

Then the Lord God formed a man from the dust of the ground and breathed into his nostrils the breath of life, and the man became a living being. Genesis 2:7

Looks like we actually are dust. You'd think that would keep us humble. *But* - we are animated dust, made alive by a wind from the breath of God.

This reminds me of the joke about the scientist and God. A scientist said to God, "We no longer need you. We can clone life, manipulate atoms, build molecules, fly through space, and do many other miraculous things. So why don't you go away and mind your own business from now on?"

God listened patiently to the man, then said, "Very well. Before I go, let's have a human-making contest."

The scientist replied, "Okay, we can handle that!"

"But," God added, "let's do this like I did back in the old days with Adam."

"Sure, no problem," the scientist said. He bent down and picked up a handful of dirt.

God wagged a finger at him and said, "Whoa! Not so fast. Get your own dirt."

Originating from God is square one in our identity. But there's more. We are fashioned intentionally as an expression of a Creator who gives us inalienable rights (good word choice T. Jefferson), a purposeful path through our own brief timeline, an eternal destination, and a royal identity.

Our founders agreed that every human being is created by God Almighty. But God goes further. He has invited us to become his children.

> Yet to all who did receive him, to those who believed in his
> name, he gave the right to become children of God -
> children born not of natural descent, nor of human decision
> or a husband's will, but born of God.
>
> John 1:12

Compare the kind of world shaped by that Biblical view to the road taken by those drifting toward a Godless universe and the world made by that view. Down one road everyone, every life matters. Down the other road, if we are only clever animals, titles become crucial. They have to carry the full weight of worth, meaning, and purpose. The more powerful the title, the more valuable the person. And vice versa. The name of the game becomes the survival of the strongest title. This view has shaped entire cultures. Emperor - Subject. Royalty - Peasant. Master - Slave. Bourgeoisie - Proletariat. Aryan - Jew. Gentry - Serf. Brahmin - Shudras. Moslem - Infidel. In those cultures, title equates to worth.

Absent a bedrock premise (a priori assumption) of a God who created all of us, some people crown themselves a little 'g' god of their own private universe. Like all of us, they are sorely in need of a visit with Job and Jesus for perspective and title clarification.

Thank God, our founders placed the Biblical view as a cornerstone of our country. "All" are created equal and endowed with self-evident rights. Granted, it took a bloody civil war and more legislation and ongoing righteous struggle to affirm and establish that. Old ways and titles die hard, but the Truth of who makes us who we are goes marching on. This inclusiveness and universal worth didn't originate with our wise founders.

For God so loved the WORLD he gave his only son,
that WHOSOEVER believes in him shall not perish,
but have eternal life. John 3:16

It doesn't get more diverse, equitable, and inclusive than that. God loves everyone. And anyone can be a whosoever. (Hey, that might make great t-shirt material: I'm a Whosover. or Whosoevers Live Forever!)

So, my crown jewels, who am I? Who are you?

Only one answer to that question makes our lives and this journey sacred. Any other answer makes this existence futile, meaningless, morality arbitrary, justice absurd, mercy needless, and hope irrelevant.

Thank God you are my children. But even better and more beautiful, you are children of God. You are blessed Whosoevers. Whatever titles you wear in this world, hold on to and live from that identity.

Sometimes, when I dropped you off at school in the morning, I would say, "Remember who you are out there." That still goes. When you head out the door today and every day for the rest of your lives, remember who and whose you are. And that everyone you meet is much more than dust in the wind.

Love, Dad

Truth vs. *Ruse*

In a time of universal deceit,
telling the truth is a revolutionary act.

George Orwell – author

My revolutionaries,

In the opening letter about the Andy Griffith episode, a clever drifter filled Opie's head with a lot of hooey. Nonsense. His approach to life was a ruse, which is a wily strategy or slick maneuver.

Like many people today (and throughout human history), the vagabond adopted an alternate view of living outside the lines, cutting corners, disregarding norms, and bendin' the law to do and get what he wanted. He even coated his ruse in a thin veneer of bravado mixed with a dash of charisma and a pound of pride. He claimed to have the courage others didn't have to live his liberated way. (See the letters: Courage vs. Bravado and Character vs. Charisma)

Of course, Opie's dad saw through the Shinola and called the drifter on it. That's what parents do until our children develop a nose to sniff out crapola on their own. As Andy put it:

"Wrong ideas come packaged with so much glitter it's hard to convince 'em that other things might be better in the long run."

Like Andy, I want you to develop a nose for the telltale odor of a ruse. To do that, you need four things.

I can't count how many times we watched The Wizard of Oz. Remember what the Scarecrow, Tin Man and Lion wanted? A pure heart. A good brain. And true courage. That's three of the four ruse sniffers you'll need. The fourth and most essential thing is a reliable measuring stick, a standard to weigh the merit of a matter against.

Take the drifter. Was his heart pure? Hardly. It was devious. He had a clever enough brain. By his own admission, he lived by his "wits." History and current culture are full of wily, silver-tongued charlatans whose compromised hearts twist their thinking to its own motives and appetites. As for true courage, the drifter counterfeited it with brazen self-centeredness. There's always been a lot of that around. And what was his measuring stick? The rule of law? The Golden Rule? Obviously not. His standard or highest authority was himself. His happiness. His desires. And his needs. (See the letter: Joy vs. Happiness) His theme song could have been *I Me Mine* by Beatle George Harrison. Give it a listen.

The same thing is true about the prodigal son in the story recorded in Luke 15. Avarice (greed) consumed his heart. He wanted stuff, via daddy's money, and he wanted it now, not tomorrow. His nagging dissatisfaction drove him to go his own way, to live a party life in rebellion to his roots and family values, all in the cause of personal freedom. That sounds like the 1960s. I know. I was there. The 1970s was same song next verse. For that matter, every decade since has added its own verse and beat to the same tune.

Substituting a ruse for truth is a pandemic. It's everywhere.

But, before I give in to the all-too-easy temptation of finger-pointing, let me add a little perspective.

My heart is compromised. My more than fairly functional brain has made choices from brazen self-centeredness, aided by a touch of charisma and a river of pride. I know the drive for independence and personal freedom. I've had moments where I lacked the courage to live and speak what I believe. And sometimes still do. Although biting my tongue in some situations could be considered a touch of good sense and self-control. There are times my theme song could have been *I Me Mine*. The plain fact is: We are all prone to be drifters and prodigals. As the old hymn Come Thou Fount says:

> Prone to wander, Lord, I feel it
> Prone to leave the God I love

So, my marvelous munchkins, beware and self-aware. Our own nature and the currents of culture have a way of carrying us away from capital T Truth.

What changes first in the drifter and prodigal? The heart or mind? What changes in any of us? To draw us away from the Truth and weaken our courage to live by it? In a world with so many influences, how do we possibly keep our heart pure, our mind focused and our courage strong?

Look at Sheriff Taylor's first beef with the drifter:

"There seems to be something wrong with Opie's thinkin'. He's gotten a little twisted on things lately, like being able to tell the difference between right and wrong."

A compromised heart with selfish motives can often lead to twisted thinking. But often, a ruse introduces a new idea by changing the language. Like "freeing" gumballs from a machine with a magic word, "Tuscarora." Instead of a coin. Only there was no magic. The drifter used sleight of hand, a distraction, and a tool to trip the mechanism in the back of the machine, releasing a gumball. Opie was amazed. Naïve. And completely sucked in.

Salespeople, marketers, politicians, and even presidents use this language ruse all the time. "No money down. Pay later." The reality: keep paying for years far beyond the value. "It's a fixer-upper with real potential." Fixer-upper can equal money pit. "We must invest in America." Invest actually means tax and spend. Or hucksters just flat out lie: "Read my lips. No new taxes." "With my plan you can keep your doctor." "The border is secure." All hooey. Even the Wizard of Oz tried to pull a fast one on Dorothy and her friends, literally with smoke and mirrors. At least he proved to be good-hearted and valiant.

Andy makes it clear, it's not just kids who find it hard to tell right from wrong. He says, "Not that that's an easy thing, there's a lot of grownups still strugglin' with that same problem."

Behind a compromised heart and twisted thinking, there's a root cause that goes deeper.

Hang in here with me for a little history fly-over. This is a broad-brush picture, but it will give you a window on the situation all around us today. And inside every one of us, too.

Long before you and me and Andy Taylor and Opie, America was founded on a standard: "All men are created equal and endowed by their Creator with certain unalienable rights." (I know,

I refer to this a lot. Because the essential truth is so central.) Behind that standard, the ultimate authority the founders based our rights and laws on is - God. For thousands of years, God was the ultimate authority in most of the world, certainly in Judeo-Christian cultures.

Farther back, beginning about 1685, there was a period called the "Enlightenment," also called the Age of Reason. Some good things came out of it. Among them, our democracy based on the value of the God-created individual. This is a core value that accounts for America's shining uniqueness. Every life is sacred.

But a perfect storm was brewing. The Romantic age, about 1800 to 1855, celebrated the individual, intuition, the human spirit and glorified the beauty of nature. The Romantic poets and authors fell in love with themselves, their intuitions (feelings) and the sound of their own voices. I know. I became enamored with them and took more courses about them than I needed. Probably because I was enamored with myself and my free-spirit, self-preoccupied state of mind. Not uncommon when we're young.

Authors Henry David Thoreau and Ralph Waldo Emerson led the charge. Thoreau believed in the inherent goodness of people and nature. He was a Pantheist, the view that nature and God are the same, not separate. Ralph Waldo Emerson promoted intuition, an individual's subjective "sense" of things, as a higher way to comprehend reality. This trickled down to my generation into hit songs. "It can't be wrong when it feels so right." *(You Light Up My Life)* "I don't care what's right or wrong." *(Help Me Make It Through the Night.)*

Nineteenth-century Romantics believed in the "divine

sufficiency of the individual." Their brand of self-reliance and optimism found an eager audience in the new America. (See the letter: Hope vs. Optimism) Poet Walt Whitman summed them up pretty well in his famous, and very long poem, *I Sing of Song of Myself.* (Read it some night when you need help getting to sleep.)

The Age of Science followed, including Charles Darwin and evolution. He and others blended science with reason, and the dots were not hard to connect. By 1883, a German atheist philosopher, Nietzsche (knee-chee), said a big idea out loud: God is dead.

What or who do you think took God's place at the center of the universe? If you said, us, the top rabbit pulled out of the evolutionary hat, you are correct.

Just in the last few hundred years, the ultimate authority has shifted away from God. Cultures have drifted and dispensed with Divine authority. (See the letter: Dignity vs. Ego) But cultures only do that because individual hearts and minds drift and mutiny against the idea of any power over and beyond us.

Now here you are, my noble navigators, in your time in the sun, the Post-Modern period. Or, as Cheryl Crow dubbed it in her song, *Every Day is a Winding Road* 1996, "Welcome to the Age of Anything Goes." Some call it Woke. Whatever the label - faith, reason, science and even common sense have taken a back seat to self as the center of the universe. Every person can make up their own rules, reality, even their own truth.

Undoubtedly, the music of my youth added its own anthems to this up-side-down world order. Catchy hits like *It's Your Thing* by the Isley Brothers. "It's your thing. Do want you want to do. I can't tell you who to sock it to." *I Gotta Be Me* "Whether I'm right or whether I'm wrong."The sappy classic, Feelings. And of course, John Lennon's *Imagine*. "Imagine there's no heaven/It's easy if you try/No hell below us/Above us only sky" (See the letter: Heaven vs. Sky) The Romantic poets and writers would have loved the groovy 60s and 70s music. "Different strokes for different folks, and so on and so on and scooby-dooby-do." (*Everyday People* by Sly and the Family Stone)

What does this history sketch have to do with us? That perfect storm is still brewing for you and me. What happened historically can easily happen inside any of us. We can little by little move away from the bedrock view of God as Creator, Designer, Moral Compass, Sustainer, Redeemer and center of the universe. Modern ideas question "old" thinking. Beliefs are recast and denounced as myths and superstitions. Even the unalienable rights of liberty and the pursuit of happiness are repurposed to erase lines about what was once clearly taboo or immoral. (See the letter: Joy vs. Happiness)

When the highest authority is replaced, the moral landscape can be rewritten. What was once wrong can become not just preferred but right, protected, voted into law, and even applauded. This is happening all around us. And it can happen inside us, too.

I said earlier, the most essential thing in spotting a ruse is having a standard to measure it against. This is my "Sheriff" Dad heads up:

Change the ultimate authority, and the heart and mind will follow.

Why do you think tyrants attempt to control education beginning with the very young? They know that by questioning and changing the highest authority, minds and hearts can be changed.

This sleight of hand is a mainstay, especially of many in power today. And goes way back before 1685. Long before Andy of Mayberry, before the Ages of Enlightenment, Romanticism, Science, Post-Modernism/Anything Goes, the Apostle Paul clearly laid out the effects of this in his time.

> For since the creation of the world God's invisible qualities—his eternal power and divine nature—have been clearly seen, being understood from what has been made, so that people are without excuse. For although they knew God, they neither glorified him as God nor gave thanks to him, but their *thinking became futile and their foolish hearts were darkened...* They exchanged the truth about God for a lie, and worshiped and served created things rather than the Creator. Romans 1: 19-21 & 25

That's a statement the size of Mount Everest about human psychology. About our inner wiring. And how belief shapes hearts and minds. The connection is not subtle. Changing the ultimate authority away from God darkens hearts and twists thinking. Get your head and heart around that!

No surprise, the Biblical point of view is now considered by a growing number to be unmodern, small-minded, bigoted and intolerant. (See the letter: Grace vs. Tolerance) Critics, committed drifters and radical prodigals are more than vocal.

The only people mad at your for telling the
truth are those living a lie.

Pravinee Hurbungs

If we are not created in the image of our Creator, if we are only the sum of our parts and nothing more, then the founders' declaration could look something like: "All people birthed fully functional are autonomous, free agents subject only to the evolving laws of the land and the survival of the fittest." In that kind of society, a tyrannical majority and the strongest would rule, right? And our original national motto could be altered from e pluribus unum, "Out of Many One," to ex nihilo gratis, "Out of Nothing for Nothing." Instead of "In God We Trust" on our money, it could read "Whoever Rules the Gold Rules."

But if we are created by Divine authority, endowed by God with certain unalienable rights, then there is a nobility beyond our remarkable biology and a Truth that prevails through every age and wind of change.

Thank God for this planet-sized nugget of wisdom:

A lie doesn't become truth, a wrong doesn't become right,
and evil doesn't become good just because it's accepted
by a majority.

Booker T. Washington

Can I get an "amen"?

In some other letters, I referred to Robert Frost's image of two roads diverging in a wood. And how life-shaping that choice is. Here's a poem I wrote for you about one of the newest Shinola

peddlers. There have always been wily communicators. But you all
have been born in a time of very sophisticated, high-tech Pied
Pipers. It's harder and harder to know what's real and true, and
who is real and true - and to choose the road that makes all the
difference.

A Tale of Two Realities

Two realities diverged in a darkening wood
of the 21st Century, and pondering I stood.
Having no second me to travel them both
I turned for guidance to the signs by the road.

Appearing on a giant LED to my left
"I am Alias and Imago" a CGI bot said.
"I am the lightning portal of the UBU revolution,
Master of imagining, perception, and illusion."

The face before me fluidly morphed
Into famous and familiar, a visual tour-de force
A Beatle, my dear father, a sweet-remembered flame,
Mesmerized, I watched them join in the refrain,

"All who take this road will sing along, eventually,
To AI Did it My Way, AI Gotta Be Me.
Truth and Free Thinking are my Achilles heel,
But I can turn the truth into just what people feel."

"Let me do the thinking, set your true self free!
Just lay down your freedom, friend, come and follow me.
See now what I did there? Surely, words aren't just for show!
Welcome to the land of Wow, where truly anything goes."

Glancing right, an aging sign bore in crimson paint
"I am Alpha and Omega." It went on to claim,
"I am life and love, the beginning and the end,
Master of now, what will be, and all that has been."

"Eventually, every soul will look up and see
The final curtain rise to unveil eternity.
I will make good in full on all that I have said,
And leave no foe unvanquished, every fear, even death."

"Blessing and trouble lie down this winding road,
But the Truth will light your way and set you free to know
Your worth, your holy mission, your glorious destiny
So, lay down your burdens here, friend, come and follow me."

I shall be telling this by and by
With dear friends remembering why - and whence
Two realities diverged in a darkening wood, and I -
I took the one more hallowed by
the One who made all the difference.

My brave hearts, it's not easy these days to discern, live and speak
the Truth. It's never been easy. Don't be surprised that when

confronted by it, the ruse will defend and excuse itself, sometimes furiously. This can fracture family ties and friendships, divide churches and countries. Historically, failing to speak and stand against the ruse has resulted in ruthless tyranny, violence, unspeakable acts and even world war!

Well, I've probably spilled more than enough ink on this. The big picture is this: All our hearts are compromised. Our thinking clouded at times. And our courage wains. Even in those of us who claim God as our highest authority. As Sheriff Taylor told the drifter, for Opie, there was a lot of "unscramblin'" to be done. The same goes for all of us. (See the letter: Savior vs. Hero)

Let me go back to these questions. In a world littered with the slick pitches of competing views, seductive pleasures and a diverse buffet of values, how do we purify our hearts, clear our minds and fuel our courage? (See the letter: Awe vs. Wow)

Look what the prodigal son did after drifting so far away. As the story goes, he "came to his senses." His thinking got unscrambled. Hunger, poverty, pain and a hollowness in his soul made him realize that being the center of the universe didn't deliver what he imagined. He remembered the blessings and stability of his father's house. And his identity in it. (See the letter: Identity vs. Title) He turned around (repented), humbled himself, and found the courage to return home. Can you imagine how anxious he was about his reception? And how sweet his relief at the joyful way his father welcomed him back home?

So, we turn and return our heart and mind to the highest authority. To the God who created us. Who gave us free will to run to the other end of the earth from him. The God who came here to make a way back home. Who loves drifters and prodigals not yet awakened to their true identity and place in the world - and in God the Father's heart. He loved us while we were drifting. And he calls us to love drifters, too, by having the courage to speak and live the truth in love. That's what Andy did to the wily hobo. It touched that drifter's soul and at the end of the episode awakened his conscience.

Above all else, guard your heart, for it is the wellspring of life.
Proverbs 4:23

Do not conform to the pattern of this world,
but be transformed by the renewing of your mind.
Then you will be able to test and approve what is
God's good, pleasing and perfect will.
Romans 12:2

This letter wouldn't be complete if, as your father, I didn't include practical ways of guarding your heart and keeping your thinking untwisted. (See the letter: Awe vs. Wow) This will sound simple. And it's easy to underestimate. These two ways to guard your heart and renew your mind have a proven track record of many centuries. Ready? This may seem underwhelming, but believe me, it's not:

God's word. And prayer.

Yep. This lengthier letter and history review all lead to this: By reading God's wisdom and heart for us and by praying, listening and practicing the ways of our Maker and Redeemer, the ruse of enticing entanglements and dark influences will become more visible. And more resistible. You will be less likely to fall prey to the shiniest, most dazzling Shinola. And you will have less unscramblin' to do than I did. That's my hope.

My dear world-shapers, did you ever think having faith in and following God would be a revolutionary thing to do? It is. Jesus was a revolutionary. And the master of speaking the Truth in love. Especially the hard truth. (See the letter: Grace vs. Tolerance) I still have a lot of growing to do in that. And a ton to learn about loving well. By the shape our world is in, we all do. But, trusting the Lord's sovereign hand on history, as well as the future, and knowing who you are, I rest easier passing the baton to you.

Love, Dad

Letter 26

Grace vs. *Tolerance*

Amazing grace, how sweet the sound.

John Newton

Tolerance is a virtue of the man without convictions.

G.K. Chesterton

My gifts of grace,

When you all were very young, five things could land you in big trouble: disobedience, disrespect, lying, stealing, and physical violence. Those things were not tolerated. Whenever you crossed one of these lines, you knew the penalty and almost always received it.

I say *almost* because sometimes, after letting you sit in your room dreading the discipline, I'd come in and sit beside you on the bed. We talked about what line you crossed. You knew you were guilty. Each time I affirmed how much I love you. Discipline was part of that love. My dad loved me in the same way.

For the Lord disciplines the one he loves,
just as a father disciplines the child in whom he delights.

Prov. 3:12

Now and then, I gave you mercy and grace by withholding what you deserved. I still remember the relief on your faces. This was meant to be an example of what God does for us. He extends mercy and grace even though we are guilty of crossing many lines.

To this day, I know you don't think the moments of grace meant your bad behavior was tolerated, right? Why? Because discipline moved the behavioral lines from theory to reality in your mind and heart (via your backside or privileges taken away). I'm glad to say none of you required a heaping helping of consequences. Maybe because discipline worked. You got the message sooner than later. I never enjoyed it. You know that. But I sure enjoy the people you're becoming.

There are powerful examples of Jesus extending mercy and grace in tense situations. The woman caught in adultery (John 8) was about to be stoned, according to Jewish law. After the crowd dropped their stones and left, he told her, "Has no one condemned you? Neither do I." Does that mean he overlooked and was tolerant of her offense? Hardly. He added, "Go and sin no more." He knew her offense. So did she. Jesus offered mercy and grace and called her to a new life. Can you imagine the woman taken in adultery resisting and dismissing the love that saved her life? And returning to her old ways?

Think of grace and tolerance like this. Gravity, like grace, is wide. It encircles the entire world, active over every inch. The power of it is absolute. Gravity is intolerant. It applies to everyone, with the possible exception of that time Jesus and Peter walked on the water. Jesus is clearly in charge of gravity and grace.

Likewise, God set up spiritual reality in a similar way. Grace is wide, but the nature of Truth and the way of salvation are narrow. The most well-known scripture in the Bible, John 3:16, shows how inclusive God is. "For God so loved the world…" But there's also this. Jesus said, "No one comes to the Father except through me." (John 14:6) Those statements have a lot of gravity to them.

Many today interpret that Biblical narrow way as the cardinal secular sin of intolerance. They understand and accept the intolerance of physical gravity. But not a spiritually narrow way. Why? Because the open-handed nature of God's love enables any heart to resist and even defy Him. We have free will.

Tolerance has become an anesthesia to blur and erase "antiquated" lines in a diverse population. Tolerance sings, "Imagine there's no more lines." (See the letter: Heaven vs. Sky) Tolerance bends society degree by degree toward more "enlightened" and "liberated" views of creation, marriage, justice, death and dying, history, morality, gender, abortion and many other basic areas of culture and civilization. Good gives way to not-so-bad. Not-so-bad gives way to a-long-way-from-good.

Here's another way to look at this.

Remember when we lived in Colorado? I loved it. Having grown up in a conspicuous absence of forests in West Texas, I recently learned an amazing thing.

Did you ever notice how all those trees in the Rocky mountains grow straight up to the sky even on steep slopes? How do they know to do that, right? It turns out, trees (and most plants) detect gravity using tiny structures within the cells of their roots and shoots called statoliths, which tell them which way is up. This capacity is known as gravitropism. (Fun words to throw into a conversation, right?

You're welcome.) A plant's growth also follows the direction from which light comes. This is called phototropism, which means seeking or bending toward the light. Like sunflowers do. (Another cool word and concept, right?) That's why all the trees in a forest grow straight up and reach for the light. How awe-mazing is that?

What happens when a person or an entire culture constantly inhales the anesthesia of tolerance and loses both senses of gravitropism and phototropism? When it no longer knows which way is up and where the light is? An Irish poet, one of my favorites, described it well.

> Things fall apart; the center cannot hold;
> Mere anarchy is loosed upon the world,
> The blood-dimmed tide is loosed, and everywhere
> The ceremony of innocence is drowned;
> The best lack all conviction, while the worst
> Are full of passionate intensity.
>
> William Butler Yeats
> from his poem *The Second Coming*

Look around. Disobedience (lawlessness), disrespect, lying, stealing and physical violence are on the rise everywhere. (Apparently, someone needs much more than a time out.) What used to be considered unholy, unnatural, immoral is now viewed by many as good, liberated, normal, and even celebrated. Much of the new reality is a break from reality. That's called psychosis. The new reality can now lean in any direction, be distorted into any shape by anyone. (See the letter: Truth vs. Ruse)

To even write these sentences, to hold this view, is considered intolerant by some, and out of sync with "modern" culture. Disagreeing with anyone's subjective reality can be regarded as bigoted hate speech. And met with passionate intensity, lawsuits, job loss, riots and even violence.

Cautions about the effects of tolerance are not new. Here is a biting, on-target statement from an author I respect and admire. He predicted most of the atrocities committed by tyrants in the 20th century.

"Tolerance will reach such a level that intelligent people will be banned from thinking so as not to offend the imbeciles."

Fyodor Dostoyevsky 1811 - 1881

Sounds like that applies in this "enlightened" century, too.

My grace-giving light-seekers, you have been born into a world where two very different roads diverge. One shaped by Grace and Truth. The other by tolerance and Shinola.

Here's the challenge. How do we live our convictions on a tilting planet in a culture no longer standing upright, where everyone is free to choose shadow instead of light? How do we extend grace to indifferent drifters, resolute rebels and defiant prodigals?

Holocaust survivor Ellie Wiesel said, "We must always take sides." At the least, this means vote our convictions. My children, DO NOT skip voting! Don't underestimate the power of your vote or voice. As the saying goes, "The only thing necessary for the triumph of evil is that good men do nothing." (Edmund Burke – Irish statesman and philosopher) We must be proactive.

But how do we apply the living water of Grace? As an antidote to the distorting effects of tolerance, Grace can help awaken tilting trees in the shadows to a new way of standing and thriving. First, we have to learn to see the trees in the forest. The way Jesus did. The way Dostoyevsky put it:

To love someone means to see them as God intended them.

That's difficult when someone is screaming in your face and threatening to harm you for your convictions. In fact, that happened to me on a street outreach with YWAM in Amsterdam. An angry man who hated Christians raged inches from my face. I expected him to hit me. My face remained calm, but on the inside I prayed feverishly. He backed off.

I bet some who took up stones to kill the adulterous woman were later among the crowd in Pilate's courtyard shouting, "Crucify him!" But even in the face of their rage, Jesus saw them as God intended them to be. With his dying breaths, he said, "Father, forgive them."

Living grace and faith out loud isn't easy. And sometimes risky. In fact, Jesus predicted resistance and gave a radical way for us to face it.

"Love your enemies and pray for those who persecute you."
Jesus – Matthew 5:44

God is merciful. His grace is wide. Mercy is *not* getting what we deserve. I know you understand that from our early discipline sessions. Grace is *getting* what we don't deserve, freedom from punishment, guilt and shame - a new life and relationship to God and others - courage beyond our own strength - and of course, salvation and ultimately heaven. No matter what lines we've crossed, God offers mercy and grace to us and everyone on the planet. That's why Grace, when it takes root in a soul, is so amazing and sounds so sweet.

My giant redwood saplings, if you are the only trees in the forest standing upright, stand. And rather than cut down the tilted trees around you, learn to speak the truth, even the hard truth, in love. Offer grace through kindness. Hardly anyone can argue with kindness. (See the letter: Kind vs. Nice) Keep growing where you're planted. Trust the Holy Spirit's gravitropism and phototropism to know true north and seek the light. And you will point others to it.

You may not see what I see in you, but truth be told, I'm already looking up to you.

Hope vs. *Optimism*

"Hope" is the thing with feathers -
That perches in the soul -
And sings the tune without the words -
And never stops - at all

Emily Dickinson

My feathered fledglings,

One of my favorite pictures of you, Wyatt, is on the cover of my album "Songs in the Key of Awe." You were nine or so. Your mom snapped it on a beach at the precise moment you jumped up toward a flock of seagulls who are all looking at you. Your head is back, arms reaching up and spread out like their wings. Your toes hang in midair, just above the sand. It looks like you're taking off to join the flock of birds.

For me, that image captures a core longing in my soul. I suppose in every human soul. (See the letter: Awe vs. Wow) That snapshot is like the space between heartbeats. It's weightless and free of any care. If I could live in that moment, I would.

But we are not lighter than air. Gravity and the next heartbeat make flight impossible. Our feet have to walk in a world that is heavy and full of challenges and troubles. Our hearts must find a way through difficulties aplenty.

I have mostly been a fairly buoyant person. By temperament, I suppose. My mother, Oteka, was that way while I was growing up. She was as happy as the sound of her Cherokee Indian name. Later, life's troubles and her inner struggles muted her joy. But as kids, she came in every morning to wake us up whistling a little tune.

Willow, you were happy and smiling the moment your eyes opened every morning. Wyatt, from the beginning, you were not a morning person. Sometimes at the breakfast table in your grogginess you would duck your head and say, "Don't see me!" That still makes me laugh. It wasn't long before your focus and determination showed itself in everything you put your mind to. Sawyer, you're like your sister, more light-hearted, a people person, and like your brother, athletic and always on the move.

You've all faced enough now, we've faced enough as a family, that you know it takes more than natural buoyancy or temperament to get through some things. Happy, healthy, hassle-free times don't require much stamina or faith. It's easy to feel upbeat about life when things are good. Easy to put on the song "Happy" by Pharrell, sing "nothin' gonna bring me down" and dance free and wild like a child.

Thank God for those times. As a brilliant friend reminded me recently, the happy, healthy, hassle-free times may be answers to prayers and what we hoped for. There really are reasons to be deliriously happy. (See the letter: Joy vs. Happiness) You three are some of my top reasons to be heaping-helping happy.

In good times, hope and optimism gather dust on the shelf… until something changes drastically or goes very wrong. In hard times, one of them works better than the other. One of them is easy to fake. The other is not.

To keep going on the dark days and long nights when the weight of trouble and heartache is too much to bear, we need something that gives us the strength to carry on. Whistling a happy tune will not do. Neither will singing "Tomorrow, Tomorrow, I love ya tomorrow. You're only a day away." In fact,

> Singing cheerful songs to a heavy heart
> is like taking someone's coat in cold weather.
>
> Proverbs 25:20

No need to sugarcoat it. Life can be excruciatingly painful. Facing it with mere optimism is like trying to hide the Grand Canyon with a band-aid.

I've faced a fistful of blows that crushed me. They left me shattered and reeling and thinking I was down for the count. I've trudged long, dark valleys. As James Taylor put it, "I've seen lonely days that I thought would never end." (from *Fire and Rain*) You know some of mine. A year after high school, I spent nine months in a body cast after major back surgery. In relationships, I've experienced betrayal, rejection, reversal and the sudden death of someone I loved and had planned to marry, before your mother. One song that came out of that challenging time is called Press On.

> I was down in the valley of the shadow of death
> Where the passion for life drained like blood from my chest
> And it took more than my will just to take a step
> When the compass of hope was gone.

On the ocean so lonesome I was not left alone
Had some heavyweight friends when my heart was a stone
and they carried the heartache and made it their own
When the currents of sorrow were strong

> *Press On* by Jim Weber and me
> from the Wind and the Wave

You are no strangers to loss either. The deaths of your Aunt Glenda and your great Aunt Annie. Both of my parents. Moving across the country twice, leaving close friends. You've had fractures and failures in relationships. Most painful of all, when your mother decided she didn't want to be married anymore, the divorce devastated us all. Including her.

I wrote a painful song for you during that storm. *Love Never Fails (though lovers do)* It's one of the hardest I've ever written.

O, dear hearts, My earth angels
Nothing means more to me than you
The bridge between your mother and me
May have washed away but here's the truth

This hurricane may darken the sky
But our love for you is high and dry
Safe above the storm it can fly
For no rhyme or good reason
Some hearts have seasons, too
Love never fails – though lovers do

That heartache couldn't simply be overcome by a positive attitude and optimism. Grabbing a ukulele in any overwhelming situation and singing "You are my sunshine, please don't take my sunshine away" can't scatter the dark clouds.

So, what can keep us from becoming cynical, dead inside or going under? There's not enough ice cream, comfort food, alcohol, drugs, pleasure, adventure or psychological gymnastics that can rescue and revive a drowning heart. I know. I've been there a few times. I've wrestled heartache so deep it made me understand why people rashly decide to quit, end it all, just to be free of the pain. Emily Dickinson understood that.

> There is a pain - so utter
> It swallows substance up
> Then covers the Abyss with Trance
>
> poem # 599

My priceless children, I hope you never suffer pain or heartache to the point it threatens to swallow you up. And keep you in a trance of sorrow. Jesus knew how hard life can be. He faced the abyss. And crossed it. He didn't sugarcoat it for us. "In this world you will have tribulation." (John 16:33) He didn't say hassles and SNAFUs. "Tribulation" covers a limitless variety of trials and suffering. Facing and overcoming them takes tying your heart to something more substantial than well-meaning motivational expressions like:

> Even the darkest night will end, and the sun will rise.
>
> Victor Hugo - Les Miserables.

Here comes the sun, doo doo doo doo

Here comes the sun, and I say, It's alright

George Harrison - Beatle

As much as I love Victor Hugo and the Beatles, counting on the sunrise as a sign that the world is still turning is not enough. Heartache is oblivious to the clock and calendar. In fact, suffering takes eloquent inspirational sayings and hit songs and flicks them like cigarette butts into the face of the sunrise. Which I did in one dark season of grief after sleepless nights.

But here's the steady light at the end of the tunnel. After the Lord warned us about tribulation, he didn't leave us hanging in the dark on that hard news. He added, "But take courage. For I have overcome the world." That's sounds sweet, like amazing grace. But how do we take courage when empty is all we're full of?

I found an essential lifeline in the depths of my deepest sorrows. It's what I pray you learn before anguish comes to your door. When you were all very young, I put it in a children's song called "Hope Rope." It asks and answers the right question.

When I'm hangin' by a thread
I'm too sad to raise my head
I'm feelin' like soggy bread
I sing this little song

Hope is a rope that keeps the heart afloat
Hope is a rope that keeps the heart afloat
Hope is a rope that keeps the heart afloat

Where do you tie your hope rope?
To the anchor of my soul
Where do you tie your hope rope?
To the rock that never rolls

I mentioned Victor Hugo. We love the story and musical Les Mis. In it, Cosette sings a song as a little girl called "Castle on a Cloud." It's about a place where "Crying at all is not allowed, not in my castle on a cloud." Willow, when you were a little girl, I painted a castle in the clouds for your purple bedroom. Of course, you always knew there was no such place in the clouds. It just represents a longing for relief from hurts and tears in this life.

When tears and misery come, we need more than inspiration. Not a pep talk or imaginary castle in the clouds. We need an incarnation. Real hope. Someone to rescue us, like Jean Val Jean rescues Cosette. (See the letter: Savior vs. Hero)

Real hope has real feet that walks the ground we walk. Our real hope is more than a hero. He was born, lived, laughed, suffered, bled, died and rose again. An old hymn says it best.

My hope is built on nothing less
Than Jesus' blood and righteousness
I dare not trust the sweetest frame
But wholly lean on Jesus' name

Even leaning on the Lord, trouble will find you. I wish I could protect you from it, from the hurt and heartache, but I can't. In fact, I assure you a day will come that breaks your heart. Yes, of course, I wrote a song for you about that.

For the Day That Breaks Your Heart

Vs1
This is a song for the day that breaks your heart
A gentle warning of unexpected scars
Wishing it won't come won't keep it away
This is a song for that day

Refrain 1:
Someone who loved you walks away
Your technicolor world melts into gray
Breathing in and breathing out becomes an act of faith
This is a song for that day

Vs 2
This is a song for a painful day ahead
But don't love cautiously or live in dread
Wishing it won't come, frozen and afraid
This is a song for that day

Refrain 2:
Someone you trust does not have your back
A bitter heart will try to widen the crack
Unless sorrow and forgiveness counterattack
This song is for a day like that

BRIDGE:
Wrap this melody around your soul
When I can't be there to hold you close
And know a heart that hurts is one that works
And lives to love another day

Vs 3
This is a song for the day you can't escape
A word of comfort to help your heart embrace
What is bound to come can shake and shape your faith
This is a song for that day

Refrain3
Someone you love runs out of days
Suddenly they're gone or gently slip away
More than ever you'll be carried by Amazing Grace
This is a song for that day

BRIDGE
Wrap this melody around your soul
When I can't be there to hold you close
And know a heart that hurts is one that works
And lives to love another day

Vs1
This is a song for the day that breaks your heart
A gentle warning of unexpected scars
I wish when it comes, I could take your place
This is a song for that day

My sacred hearts, if I can be there for you on those days, I will. But whether I can or not, the Lord has promised to be there. He predicted hard days. And he can not only make a way through but a way back to life. I know that from living it. (Wrote that song, too, but I'll wrap this up.)

He predicted something else. That there is a place beyond the clouds where "He will wipe away every tear... and there will be no more death or sorrow or crying or pain." (Revelation 21:4) Until then, we are assured that -

> ... suffering brings about perseverance; and perseverance,
> character; and character, hope; and hope does not disappoint,
> because the love of God has been poured out within our
> hearts through the Holy Spirit who was given to us.
>
> Romans 5: 3-5

Of course, the journey from suffering through perseverance to character and hope is easier read than endured.

So, when tribulation and heartaches come, and they will, keep your hope rope tied to the anchor of your soul who walked this painful road himself. Lean on your heavyweight friends. And hold on. Enduring and waiting for this to happen will be worth it – the thing with feathers that perches in your soul will clear its throat, take a deep breath – and sing again.

Love, Dad

Letter 28

Awe vs. *Wow*

He who can no longer pause to wonder and stand rapt in awe,
is as good as dead; his eyes are closed.

Albert Einstein

My awe-mazing children,

Remember our trip to Mount Rushmore? I have a picture of you three standing in front of it. The four giant faces carved in the side of that mountain can make anyone say, "Wow!" What a marvel. What a huge undertaking. It took fourteen years to complete! It's understandable why those presidential faces stand out in history. They were monumental men, did monumental things. They deserve honoring. And Mount Rushmore deserves the wow.

But the faces in that photo that fill me with awe are yours.

So, what's the difference between awe and wow? I'm glad you asked.

Wow can fill seats. Awe can fill our deep places.

Wow can transfix. Awe transforms.

Wow fades. Awe endures.

Wow touches our senses. Awe touches our spirits.

Wow can be manufactured and marketed. Awe transcends hype. Wow delivers a passing high. Awe delivers accrued joy and shalom.

Maybe some examples would better paint a picture.

Wow is shaking Ringo's hand. And Margaret Thatcher's. Which I did.

Awe is holding your tiny hands right after you were born. Witnessing your births was beyond words. Beyond wow. It was an awe I can't describe without shouting, weeping and singing. And writing a song, of course, which says:

> Naked arrival, primordial scream
> You're a beautiful bloom
> From the garden of your grandmother Eve
> Made by your Maker, like a clock with a soul
> And there's a fingerprint of his
> Tattooed on your chromosomes.

Welcome to the Lovely Ride

Wow is Hoover Dam.

Awe is the Grand Canyon.

Wow is standing on top of the Duomo in Florence, Italy or Freedom Tower in New York City.

Awe is standing in Anne Frank's hiding place in Amsterdam, touching the same faucet she used. Or at the site of the Lord's crucifixion in the Holy Sepulcher in Jerusalem.

Wow is solar panels. Humans finally figured out how to turn sunlight into energy.

Awe is photosynthesis. Green plants have been doing that for eons.

Wow is listening to the timeless music of the Beatles, Motown, Brahms and Chopin.

Awe is taking out your earbuds to hear the rhythm of crickets under a tapestry of a billion stars that "pour forth speech." (As songwriter King David put it in Psalm 91:1) I did this at fifteen at a church camp in West Texas. Sitting alone one night on a picnic table, I heard God whisper to my soul, "You are mine." I've carried that awe with me all my life.

Do you detect a pattern here? Humans are very clever. We innovate and build lots of wow things, mostly from materials we didn't create. On a completely different level: Sun. Sky. Water. Earth. Nature. Time. All were spoken into being. That is power beyond our reach. The wow of voice-activated lights and gadgets doesn't compare with speaking things into existence.

And how about us? We were formed by the hands of God from the dust he spoke into existence! His breath made us alive! That's enough to awe every person on the planet. Sadly, many don't get that yet.

Remember the joke I talked about in the letter Identity vs. Title? It applies here, too. A scientist approached God, said, "Listen God, we've decided we don't need you anymore. These days we can do all sorts of things that used to be considered miraculous."

God replied, "OK. Let's have a competition to see who can make a human being."

The scientist agreed and bent down to scoop up a handful of dirt.

But God said, "Whoa! Not so fast. Get your own dirt."

We can't out wow or out awe God.

When I was your age, it was all about the wow. Not much has changed. It's all about bright lights, red carpets, groovier music, faster cars, hotter looks, going viral. People still try to out wow each other. Athletes, entertainers and politicians compete for a market share with ever bigger wow - to sell tickets, fill seats and get votes. Even many churches buy into the power of wow, choosing production over anointing. Trading awe for wow.

Some wow is not without value or nutrients for the soul. I've had many wonderful wow moments.

Seeing up close, from mere feet, paintings by Van Gogh and Rembrandt in Amsterdam, and the Mona Lisa in Paris. Walking through the coliseum in Rome. The Parthenon in Athens. Viewing Mark Twains' handwriting in the library at the University of Texas. And AA Milne's original drafts of Winnie the Pooh at Cambridge University in England. Twice seeing Paul McCartney in concert. Hearing my name called to win song of the year for Via Dolorosa.

Rich wows, for sure. But here are some of my awe moments.

Witnessing each of your births. That bears repeating.

Cradling you in my arms as the sun came up when you were babies.

Rocking and singing you to sleep with you over my shoulder. Willow, when I stopped singing, you tapped my shoulder to keep going with songs like this. Which I sang to each of you.

> Where do I, Where do I
> Go when I'm afraid?
> Who is there, Who is there
> Listening when I pray?

How can I, How can I
Cross a stormy sea?
My Heavenly Father is
Watching over me

Sail away, goodnight,
Sail away, goodnight
Sail Away by me

Being baptized as a teenager on the same day with my brothers and sisters, and again symbolically many years later in the Jordan river in Israel.

Soaking my feet in the stream of En Gedi where David hid from King Saul and wrote many songs/Psalms.

Singing Via Dolorosa on the Via Dolorosa.

Using a hammer and chisel to chip pieces from the Berlin wall, experiencing history firsthand and the awe of those who defeated the tyranny that built it. (I'll put a piece in your Christmas stockings.)

Willow, watching you record for the first time when you were five. Remember the song? You nailed it on your first take!

May the Lord bless and keep you
By his Spirit guide your way
Make his face to shine on you
And be gracious unto you, I pray
  Benediction from Soundtrack of My Soul

Wyatt, standing outside your bedroom door so many times listening to you practice the drums with such passion and freedom. Watching you play djiembe in the studio on the song *Thank You, Lord.* You nailed it!

Sawyer, hearing the cheers of the crowd every time you did a back flip after scoring a soccer goal. You always nailed it!

My three indelibles, in this life you will have moments of awe but also awful moments. You will get the blues. And worse. Some things will happen that turn your soul black and blue. You've already had a few. You know some of my devastating blows. More than a few songs came from them.

In a darkness so black that I wished for the blues
Every desperate prayer seemed like heaven refused
And some days I found faith meant just tying my shoes
And it was all I could do to press on.

Press On by Jim Weber and me

Wow cannot cure the blues. It can numb or suppress them. Wow cannot rescue you from a dark night of the soul. But awe can help cure the blues. And lead us back to the light.

Thoreau wrote in 1854 that "the mass of men lead lives of quiet desperation." Today, there is even more of that, and it's often a very loud, toxic desperation. Clearly, a steady, ever more impressive diet of modern wow has not cured widespread desperation. Almost everyone chases wow. But hearts are starved for awe. A daily diet of it is part of the cure. But it takes choosing.

Time is the only coin of life.
Only you can determine how it will be spent.

Carl Sandburg – American poet

My dear clocks with souls, we can spend our precious, fleeting time chasing wow all around this planet. Of course, having some marvelous adventures is great fun, and much of it is rich. But most wow is mostly candy. Junk food. We need more than that. You might say, and I will, if Jesus is the bread of life, awe is the meat, cheese, mustard, lettuce, tomato, pickle, baked beans, potato salad and sweet tea – for the soul.

My hope is you learn to sort out wow from awe, and to seek, sup and savor awe as you go – for the sake of your soul.

So, how is that done? Glad you asked.

We know when we're hungry, right? A stomach sends signals. But we don't always recognize when our soul is hungry. We can go quite a long time on the energy snacks of wow, unaware that our soul is starving. Just like there are sources of fiber, protein, vitamins and minerals in our physical diet to keep us healthy, there are sources of awe for our souls. You might say, and I will, one of the main nutrients for the soul is awe.

One aim of this letter is to point you to sources of it. Here are some sure-fire ones I've found.

First, Jesus said we cannot live by bread alone, but "by every word that comes from the mouth of God." So, no surprise, a major source of awe is the Bible. Its pages are a banquet of revelations, realities and Truth. Here is just some of the feast it serves up.

A God who made us (Genesis 1, 2, and Psalm 139), calls us by name (Isaiah 43:1), loves us (Isaiah 43: 3), delights in us (Psalm 18:19), knows us intimately (Psalm 139), promises a future and hope (Jeremiah 29:11), defeated death (2 Luke 24;6,7), saves us (John 3:16), transforms us (Romans 8:29), gives us purpose (Ephesians 2:10), is always with us (Matthew 28:20), and will one day take us to be with him forever (1 Thessalonians 4:17).

Another rich source of awe: the beauty of nature. Even those who believe there is no Creator get a boost, a beneficial infusion from nature. Which reminds me of a cartoon of two snowmen. One says to the other, "Don't be silly. Nobody made us. We just evolved from snowflakes."

Get outside! Often. Experience the wonder, beauty, the intricate design of the Designer of our planet. From a lightning bug to the aurora borealis, "God's invisible qualities, his eternal power and divine nature, have been clearly seen, being understood from what he has made." (Romans 1:20)

> The world will never starve for want of wonders;
> but only for want of wonder.
>
> G.K. Chesterton

This naturally leads me to you, my wonders. Look in the mirror. Or just look at your hands. How many functions are involved in just holding a fork, twirling it in spaghetti, bringing it to your mouth, and getting all of it in? Or scooping ice cream? We've had plenty of practice at that. Reaching out to hold another hand? Blowing (or picking) your nose? We are "fearfully and wonderfully made." (Psalm 139:14)

Once we get over what we perceive as irregularities or flaws, (like the way I got short-sheeted on eyebrows), the fact that we simply exist should blow our minds. That we are made in God's image is like swallowing the ocean. Too vast to grasp. The only appropriate responses are awe and its heart-softening cousin, gratitude.

Other sources of awe: worship, serving others (See the letter: Usie vs. Selfie), creativity, music, art, being in love (See the letter: True Love vs. Infatuation), making babies, cooking and savoring great food, the love and company of family and dear friends, our treasured "tribe."

About music, in particular, I can't begin to list the artists and songs that fed my soul. So, I won't here. We share many of those. And you have your own list.

A treasure map to find awe wouldn't be complete without one more source where I've found it - in the revelations, realities and sacred Truths in the writings of other awe seekers. Many writers have led me to awe. For the nourishment of your souls (and a richer option than screen time), here is my short list, in no particular order. (See the letter: Reading vs Screen Time)

The Velveteen Rabbit
The Lion, the Witch and the Wardrobe
all The Chronicles of Narnia
The Adventures of Huckleberry Finn

A Tale of Two Cities
Catcher in the Rye
Diary of Anne Frank
Emily Dickinson's poetry
1984
Man's Search for Meaning
Crime and Punishment
Mere Christianity
To Kill a Mockingbird
Les Miserables

My monumental miracles, you are my personal Mount Rushmore. You don't need to wow me. Impress me. Be good at what I'm good at. I'm in awe of you. Period. Always have been. Always will be.

I witnessed your first breaths. Heard your first cries. Saw your first steps. Heard your first words. Your mother and I fed you until you could feed yourselves. You became self-feeders. The same is true with your soul. Once you have wings and are able to fly away, you can feed or neglect your soul. The reality is, an army of Shinola peddlers will always have wow to sell and distract you from doing that.

Remember, you don't have to wait till an empty, muted or lonely feeling comes, or the blues creep in and no amount of wow can chase them away. When that happens, and it will, it's a sign your soul is hungry. Go to the trusted sources of awe.

One last thought. C.S. Lewis had such a fresh way of looking at things. He said,

"You don't *have* a soul. You are a soul. You have a body."

My winged wonders, feed them both. But because we *are* souls, all the more reason to feed your soul. Feed yours daily and well. On a steady diet of awe.

In awe of you,

Love, Dad

P.S.

My dear children,

Willow, when you turned thirteen, I wrote a song called Fly Away. I sensed the time with you, and Wyatt right behind you, ticking away. Sawyer, your later arrival meant more time on our clock, but your launch day was coming. That's how life works. Time passes silently, like a balloon on the breeze. Before you know it you're many miles from where someone let go of the string.

How could I not remember?
I bless the day I saw your face
How my heart flew away
Dancing around in circles
Your feet on mine the wonder years
Where did they disappear?

CHORUS
In the blink of an eye
You grew colors like a butterfly

Waiting to fly away
Like a song I could hear
And the melody was clear
You're meant fly away

You've got your mother's beauty
And I hope the better part of me
The circle is not complete
There's a *boy* you will meet
He'll be looking for his destiny
And your heart will fly away
You will know that you know
When the time will come to go
You've got to fly away…fly away

How could I not remember?
I bless the day I saw your face
My heart still flies away
You're gonna fly away
I want you to fly

Just a handful of years later, your mother and I drove you to college. We stood at the elevator in your dorm putting off the goodbye. The door glided closed. The world changed forever. Your mother and I drove ten hours back home in mild shock at the tick tock. A year later, Wyatt, you followed your sister. My heart couldn't catch up to reality. I processed it in the usual way. Wrote a song, of course. Called Only the Heart.

Vs1

When I was boy I wanted to be a man

Now that I am, I envy the boy when

Summer went on forever

Now seasons all run together

Can't get my feet on the ground

To stop - this merry-go-round

CHORUS

Can't seize the day in my hands

Or keep the sun from setting again

Can't make this tick tock world stop turning

Can't tell the moon not to wane

Child not to grow - Cloud don't you rain

I can't get a grip on this – time passing thing

Can't ask a bird not to sing

Long for the sky, don't use your wings

Only the heart can hold such things

And the beat goes on.

I confessed in the opening letter, Sacred vs. Shinola, I am a dad with feet of clay. I sometimes settled for less than the sacred choice. That's why in all things, I hope as time glides on you will choose better, wiser, sooner, than I did, and reap the blessings and benefits of:

– Living by faith, come what may

– Enjoying the admiration of your peers (and choosing friends you admire)

– Showing true courage

– Tasting the sweetness of life (making your own ice cream)

– Experiencing lasting joy

– Finding significance

– Being kind

– Celebrating Christmas in your heart and home

– Becoming someone's hero (besides mine)

– Looking out for others

– Nurturing your inner beauty

– Seeking wisdom beyond knowledge

– Building the rebar of your character

– Leading by example and humility

– Remembering your worth and where it comes from

– Forgiving and seeking forgiveness

– Finding true love and intimacy

– Hoping in invisible certainties

– Feeding your soul

– And being blessed like I am, with children who outshine you.

All of the above are not about you meeting my expectations. Probably no surprise to you, that reminds me of a song. Remember this one? All of the Above? The recording starts with you two, Willow and Wyatt, arguing about who's the best.

What do I see when I look at you?

What stands out from my point of view?

(a) Your electric smile

(b) A heart free and wild

(c) What I've been dreamin of - or

(d) all of the above

CHORUS

It's E Z, F-ortless

And Gee, no need to guess, U C

It's really not that tough

It's L-ementary

Like LMNOP to me

The answer's obvious

You're all of the above

All of the Above by Cyndy Morgan & me

from Soundtrack of My Soul

Please, understand. This list and these letters are not boxes to check. I love you. Period. As I've told you, I don't always live up to these things and sometimes settled for less. I can still be captive to screen time instead of richer options. I have less than charitable thoughts, waste time and heart space revisiting old wounds and what ifs. I have blue days. And can lack courage, wisdom and grace. This is not about measuring up. It's about experiencing a fuller measure of what life can offer - which is what God gave me with you.

Summing it all up, friends, I'd say you'll do best by filling your minds and meditating on things true, noble, reputable, authentic, compelling, gracious—the best, not the worst; the beautiful, not the ugly; things to praise, not things to curse. Put into practice what you learned from me, what you heard and saw and realized. Do that, and God, who makes everything work together, will work you into his most excellent harmonies.

Paul - Philippians 4:8,9 MSG

My little birds, remember the episode of Andy Griffith where Opie unintentionally kills a mama sparrow with his slingshot? (Season 4/Episode 1, "Opie the Birdman") She left three little orphan chicks. Opie took on the job of raising them. He named them Wynken, Blynken and Nod. It becomes obvious they had outgrown their cage.

Andy reminds Opie there's only one more thing left to do, "Let 'em go. Let 'em be on their own. And be free. Like they was intended to be."

Opie counters, "But what if they can't fly away? Maybe I didn't do all the right things."

I know that feeling. I hope I did enough right things to give you wings.

After the young birds fly off successfully, Opie is a little sad and says, "Cage looks awful empty, don't it, Pa?"

I know that feeling, too. But here's the heart-warming finale.

Andy agrees, "Yes, son, it sure does." Then looking up, surrounded by the cheerful chirping of birds, he adds, "But don't the trees seem nice and full?"

And so is my heart, knowing you are prepared to fly into the world, to be on your own and free, like you were intended to be.

My most excellent harmonies, from the day you were each

born, I put you in bigger hands. I still do. And since I can have the last word in ink in our ongoing debate… I will.

You're the best.

Love, your grateful Dad

ABOUT THE AUTHOR

William Luz Sprague was born in Tulsa, Oklahoma, to Bill and Oteka Sprague. He grew up in West Texas, in Amarillo and Borger. He was graduated from Texas Christian University, studied literature at the University of Texas for two years before spending a quarter of a century writing songs and recording in Nashville. His favorite title is "Dad" to a daughter and two sons, his "muses with faces."

Billy Sprague is an award-winning songwriter, recording artist, and author. Previous titles include:

Letter to a Grieving Heart, a best-selling resource for those facing grief.

Ice Cream as a Clue to the Meaning of the Universe, later titled, *Is God Really There? (and is He Good?)* An autobiographical journey about the sweet and bitter of life, love and faith.

Music City Mayhymn, his debut novel, follows Nashville ace homicide detective Max Malone as he pursues a self-righteous vigilante playing judge, jury and cunning executioner of targets in high and low places.

Untamable, Billy's second novel, paints the panoramic life story of a child prodigy classical pianist set in the madness of 1930s Germany and her epic romance forged in the crucible of WW2.

Find other works at billyspraguemusic.com

MUSIC ADDENDUM
SONG PLAYLIST

The songs listed here are referred to and sometimes quoted in the letters. Use the Spotify QR code to listen as a kind soundtrack. Most titles can be found wherever you source music. My songs and *Letter to a Grieving Heart* available at: billyspraguemusic.com. Novels and non-fiction on Amazon and wherever fine books are sold.

When Nothing's Sacred Letter 1	Billy Sprague from "the Wind & the Wave"
Andy Griffith Show theme song Letter 2	Earle Hagen & Herbert Spencer
Have Yourself a Merry Little Christmas Letter 7	Ralph Blane and Hugh Martin
Almost Cut My Hair Letter 8	Crosy, Still, Nash & Young
Call Me Maybe Letter 10	Carly Rae Jepsen
O, Holy Night *Joy to the World* *Amazing Grace* Letter 11	Placide Cappeau & Adolphe Adam, 1847 Isaac Watts in 1719 John Newton in 1782

We Don't Need Another Hero	Tina Turner
I Still Need a Savior	Billy Sprague from Songs in the Key of Awe
Letter 12	
It's Your Thing	the Isley Brothers
What Have You Done for Me Lately	Janet Jackson
Your Love	The Outfield
Letter 14	
Love the One You're With	Stephen Stills
The Rose	Amanda McBroom - sung by Bette Midler
Letter 15	
Come Thou Fount	Robert Robinson at age 22 in 1758
Letter 19	
The Heart of the Matter	Don Henley, Mike Campbell, John David Souther
Letter 20	
How Will I Know	Whitney Houston
Love Songs and Fairy Tales	Cam Monroe, Joe Beck & Billy Sprague feat. Cam Newton
Forever Love	Joe Beck & Billy Sprague, feat. Michele Winters
Letter 21	
Imagine	John Lennon
This Life	Billy Sprague from Soundtrack of My Soul
I Can Only Imagine	Bart Millard and Mercy Me
Letter 24	
I Me Mine	George Harrison & the Beatles
Help Me Make it Through the Night	Kris Kristofferson, feat. Rita Coolidge
Every Day is a Winding Road	Sheryl Crow, Brian Macleod & Jeffrey Trott
I Gotta Be Me	Sami Davis Jr.

Feelings	Albert Morris & Louis Gaste
Everyday People	Sly and the Family Stone
I Did It My Way	Jacques Revaux & Paul Anka, sung by Frank Sinatra

Letter 26

Happy	Pharrell
Fire and Rain	James Taylor
Press On	Jim Weber & Billy Sprague from the Wind & the Wave and Songs to a Grieving Heart
Love Never Fails (though lovers do)	Billy Sprague
Here Comes the Sun	George Harrison & the Beatles
Hope Rope	Billy Sprague
My Hope is Built on Nothing Less	Edward Mote 1834

Letter 27

Welcome to the Lovely Ride	Billy Sprague from Soundtrack of My Soul
Sail Away	Billy Sprague also recorded by Go Fish on Superstar
Via Dolorosa	Niles Borup & Billy Sprague from Soundtrack of My Soul
Benediction	Billy Sprague from Soundtrack of My Soul
Thank You, Lord	Billy Sprague from Songs in the Key of Awe

PS

All of the Above	Billy Sprague & Cyndy Morgan from the Soundtrack of My Soul